At Issue

DNA Databases

Other books in the At Issue series:

At Issue

⏐DNA Databases

Lauri R. Harding, Book Editor

GREENHAVEN PRESS
A part of Gale, Cengage Learning

GALE
CENGAGE Learning™

Detroit • New York • San Francisco • New Haven, Conn • Waterville, Maine • London

Christine Nasso, *Publisher*
Elizabeth Des Chenes, *Managing Editor*

© 2007 Greenhaven Press, a part of Gale Cengage Learning.

For more information, contact:
Greenhaven Press
27500 Drake Rd.
Farmington Hills, MI 48331-3535
Or you can visit our Internet site at http://www.gale.com

Articles in Greenhaven Press anthologies are often edited for length to meet page require-ments. In addition, original titles of these works are changed to clearly present the main thesis and to explicitly indicate the author's opinion. Every effort is made to ensure that Greenhaven Press accurately reflects the original intent of the authors. Every effort has been made to trace the owners of copyrighted material.

LIBRARY OF CONGRESS CATALOGING-IN-PUBLICATION DATA

DNA Databases / Lauri R. Harding, book editor.
    p. cm. -- (At issue)
  Includes bibliographical references and index.
  ISBN-13: 978-0-7377-3599-4 (hardcover)
  ISBN-10: 0-7377-3599-6 (hardcover)
  ISBN-13: 978-0-7377-3600-7 (pbk.)
  ISBN-10: 0-7377-3600-3 (pbk.)
  1. DNA data banks--Law and legislation--United States--Juvenile literature. 2. DNA fingerprinting--Law and legislation--United States--Juvenile literature. 3. DNA fingerprinting--Government policy--United States--Juvenile literature. 4. Criminal justice, Administration of--United States--Juvenile literature. 5. Crim-inals--United States--Identification--Juvenile literature. 6. Privacy, Right of--United States--Juvenile literature. I. Harding, Lauri R.
  KF9666.5.D64 2007
  363.25'6--dc22
                                                2007006555

Printed in the United States of America
2 3 4 5 6 7 12 11 10 09 08

Contents

Introduction

There's no turning back now. History teaches that once a daring technology appears on the horizon—for example, nuclear power, animal cloning, stem cell research, genetically modified foods—the most humanity can do is strive to keep it in the hands of responsible people. The hope for their stewardship is that they will bring such powerful technology to its full potential without stimulating improper, illegal, or harmful use.

So it is with the formidable power of DNA technology. The genetic string of molecular wonder scientifically known as deoxyribonucleic acid (DNA) is found in every human being. Each person has a unique set of DNA sequencing (contained in body cells) that dictates that individual's physical characteristics and identity, as well as storing heredity information that passes from one generation to the next. DNA samples are generally obtained from a donor's blood, urine, saliva, or other body fluid, but may be obtained in as remote a sample as that left behind on a cigarette butt or lip print on a drinking glass. The ability to identify a person by his or her DNA carries a certainty generally greater than 99.9 percent (depending upon quality of sample and type of test done). Moreover, stored DNA samples do not degrade or degenerate over time, as do most hair, skin, or tissue samples.

For these and other reasons, DNA technology has enjoyed a widening arena of application in many scientific disciplines. The most popularized has been in the field of forensic science, where it is used to identify criminal suspects or aid in antiterrorism efforts. DNA identification (genetic fingerprinting) also has been instrumental in determining paternity and inheritance rights and for identifying remains in mass casualty situations. Studying DNA mutations and sequencing has greatly advanced the sciences of historical anthropology and ecological biology, where geneticists can learn or trace the history of particular populations. Another burgeoning field is genetic engineering, where scientists have learned to isolate, manipulate (recombine), or otherwise modify human DNA, with the hope of someday eliminating human disease or conditions caused by mutated genes.

With the ever-expanding use of DNA technology a number of issues arise. Where does society safely store all this personal data? Who should control access or use of DNA data? How long should personal DNA information be stored? And whose or which personal DNA data should be included in any DNA databanks or databases? Finally, there is the element of human error or misuse—the specific factor that can limit a technology from becoming truly indispensible science.

Take, for example, the case of Steven Avery, released from a Wisconsin prison in 2003 after serving 18 years for a 1985 sexual assault that DNA evidence later showed he did not commit. A poster child for the Wisconsin Innocence Project, Avery became an instant media darling and spokesperson for the innocent. In early 2005 he appeared with Wisconsin governor Jim Doyle to promote the recently passed Avery Bill, designed to prevent other innocents from going to prison.

A few months later, Avery was arrested and charged with the October 2005 murder of a Twenty-Five-year old female photographer, reported missing after being assigned to take pictures for *Auto Trader* magazine at the Avery family's auto salvage yard. Investigators subsequently discovered charred human bones and teeth in a burn pit at the salvage yard, along with her car. They also found her car key in the bedroom of Avery's trailer. Using the very same DNA technology that had freed Avery from prison in 2003, investigators now discovered Avery's DNA on the car key, along with his blood (and the victim's blood) in her car.

But that wasn't the end of this DNA story. Prior to the commencement of Avery's 2007 murder trial, defense lawyers accused prosecutors of "framing" Avery by planting his DNA, saved and stored from an 11-year-old blood sample taken in 1995 and later used to exonerate him in 2003. This accusation serves to bring into focus some key arguments surrounding the banking and storage of personal DNA data. A conviction of Avery for the 2005 murder, burning, and mutilation of the photographer would show the value of DNA databases, which still contained data from Avery's earlier sample. On the other hand, an acquittal might show the world that even DNA evidence can be misused by authorized officials.

The collection and storage of personal DNA information is an issue that affects everyone. *At Issue: DNA Databases* endeavors to present some of the more significant viewpoints surrounding the cutting-edge field of DNA technology.

1

What Are the Benefits and Burdens of DNA Databases?

Christine Rosen

Christine Rosen is a senior editor of the New Atlantis *and resident fellow at the Ethics and Public Policy Center.*

The use of DNA databases to free persons from death row, track down sexual partners for transmitting HIV, or deny someone insurance coverage or employment was once considered within the realm of Hollywood sci-fi. It now looms on the horizon. Much such use has already happened. But focusing on the dramatic extremes of such a significant technology undermines the full significance and inherent dangers of its capabilities. Key concerns of privacy, misuse, and human error remain inadequately addressed. Before proceeding further down this path, participants in the DNA revolution must pause to consider the potential they may unwittingly release.

Imagine the following scenario: You happen to match the physical description of a serial burglar who has been preying recently upon residents of a suburb of Richmond, Virginia. After being brought in for questioning by the police, you are asked to participate in a line-up, whereupon an eyewitness identifies you as the culprit. The police place you under arrest. The next day, the real burglar is apprehended, and you are freed—a simple case of mistaken identity. But you will have left something behind: your DNA, which the police have taken from you at arrest and stored in the state's criminal database in the form of a DNA "fingerprint."

Christine Rosen, "Liberty, Privacy, and DNA Databases," *The New Atlantis*, spring 2003, pp. 37–52. Reproduced by permission.

Or consider this: Like thousands of other Americans, you voluntarily donate a DNA sample to a large medical research study, assured by the directors of the study that your information will remain anonymous, your genetic privacy secured in an unbreakable DNA database accessed only by approved researchers. A few months later you are placed under arrest for attempted murder; one of your former sexual partners has tested positive for HIV, and you are charged with knowingly infecting her with the virus. The evidence for this charge? The supposedly anonymous DNA sample you gave to the medical researchers, which the police tracked down and tested for evidence of HIV.

Or perhaps you are like the woman whose mother and aunt both suffered from breast cancer. Wanting to know her genetic risk for the disease, she sent in a blood sample to a private lab to be DNA-tested for the mutant genes—BRCA1, BRCA2, and BRCA3—that have been found to increase a woman's risk of breast cancer by as much as sixteen times. The company that performed the test assured her that her sample would remain anonymous, the results known only to her, although the disclaimer she signed offered few specifics about these privacy protections. Four years later, she is denied insurance coverage. Why? The insurance company purchased the private lab's DNA database, ostensibly for research purposes, and cross-referenced it with its own. They red-flagged the names of people who had been tested for breast cancer.

Such scenarios carry the whiff of mediocre Hollywood screenplays, but they are closer to truth than fiction. Beginning in 2003, anyone arrested for a felony in the state of Virginia must relinquish a DNA sample for the state's forensic database. The second scenario actually happened in Scotland, where a prisoner who had voluntarily offered a DNA sample for research, on the condition that his identity remain anonymous, was later prosecuted for knowingly infecting a woman with HIV; the evidence used to prosecute him came from the supposedly anonymous sample he contributed to the research study, which prosecutors decoded and introduced in the trial. The final example is hypothetical, but the architecture is already in place for it to become a reality.

Quantum Leaps

Fifty years have passed since [James] Watson and [Francis] Crick discovered the structure of DNA, and the double helix has replaced the caduceus as the symbol of scientific and medical progress. We have mapped the human genome and embarked on identifying and curing heretofore intractable genetic conditions. With startling swiftness we have also constructed DNA databases and storage banks to manage the genetic information generated by these discoveries. The most zealous advocates for these new technologies imagine only the endless possibilities: We will solve and deter crime; we will rescue the falsely convicted from prison sentences or execution; we will uncover our genetic ancestry; we will map, understand, and cure dreaded diseases; we will tailor pharmaceuticals according to each individual's genetic make-up; we will gain crucial understanding about the respective role of nature and nurture in shaping human identity; and we will create the "genetic economy of the future."

Limited Public Awareness

So far, the public discussion of DNA fingerprinting has focused largely on its uses within the criminal justice system. In the U.S., the first criminal conviction based on DNA evidence came in 1987. The battles in the late 1980s and early 1990s over the effectiveness and accuracy of DNA as forensic evidence—infamously featured in the televised murder trial of O. J. Simpson—proved in the end to be merely a splendid little war. Courts quickly embraced DNA evidence as legally admissible, and legislatures were soon responding to law enforcement's claims that they needed DNA databases to manage this new and powerful form of forensic information. Within ten years of that first conviction, all fifty states required convicted felons to submit DNA samples; soon every state had established its own criminal DNA database.

The coming age of DNA technology will change the character of human life, both for better and for worse, in ways that we are only beginning to imagine.

In 1994, the DNA Identification Act established a national DNA database, run by the FBI, called CODIS (Combined DNA Identification System), which links all state databases. Today, the newspapers regularly bring stories of a murderer identified through a "cold hit" on a DNA database, or an innocent man freed from prison after DNA evidence exonerates him. In March 2003, Attorney General John Ashcroft announced a new initiative, "Advancing Justice Through DNA Technology," that seeks $1 billion over the next five years to aid in "realizing the full potential of DNA technology to solve crime and protect innocent people." Media coverage focused on the initiative's efforts to eliminate the backlog of DNA samples at state and federal criminal laboratories, but the initiative seeks something else as well: the expansion of CODIS. The Bush administration is keen on giving the FBI access to the full range of samples in state DNA databases—including those of people placed under arrest but not convicted—rather than the smaller range of samples currently included.

But in focusing so much on dramatic stories of finding the guilty and freeing the innocent—or the prospect of using genetic information to cure disease—we risk obscuring the full significance and inherent dangers of DNA technology. While the creation of DNA databases often can be defended case-by-case, the development of this technology serves an end in itself apart from any particular application. It provides an inescapable means of identification, categorization, and

13

profiling, and it does so with a type of information that is re-velatory in a way few things are. As bioethicist George Annas put it, DNA is a person's "future diary." It provides genetic in-formation unique to each person; it has the potential to reveal to third parties a person's predisposition to illnesses or behav-iors without the person's knowledge; and it is permanent in-formation, deeply personal, with predictive powers. Taken to-gether, the coming age of DNA technology will change the character of human life, both for better and for worse, in ways that we are only beginning to imagine—both because of what it will tell us for certain and what it will make us believe. To know one's own future diary—or to know someone else's—is to call into question the very meaning and possibility of hu-man liberty. . . .

Big Questions

At least three big questions, however, have not been adequately addressed. First, the evidence of DNA's effectiveness as a crime-fighting tool is at once impressive and ambiguous, depending on how the genetic information is used. *DNA evidence*, when used to incriminate or exonerate suspects already identified by more traditional police work, is extraordinarily useful. "Our forensic scientists can identify an individual from objects such as a half-eaten chicken sandwich, urine in the snow . . . or even cross-transfer of DNA from a handshake," [Dr. Paul] Fer-rara recently boasted to Congress. But the verdict is less clear when it comes to *DNA databases*, which attempt to match DNA evidence found at the crime scene with preexisting DNA records. *USA Today* recently reviewed the criminal DNA data-base system and found wide variations in effectiveness from state to state. Even worse, officials do not in fact know how many of the "cold hits"—the unexpected matches made when a law enforcement official plugs evidence from old, unsolved cases into a database—end in actual convictions. No one is tracking what happens once a DNA database match is made.

"We try to track cold hits to conviction," Paul Ferrara says, "but we really have not had the opportunity or resources to really study and follow statistically the actual impact." In effect, state legislatures, impressed by stories of "cold hits," are being persuaded to expand these databases with no real statistical evidence as to their effectiveness in ultimately convicting criminals.

One person's "junk" DNA might prove to be another's future wealth of information about genetic conditions.

Second, the claims by proponents of DNA databases that the genetic information used for DNA fingerprints is merely "junk DNA"—hence not capable of revealing an individual's genetic predispositions—is not the whole truth. Buried in a genetics journal from a few years ago is a report by a team of British scientists that "the standard DNA fingerprints used by police around the world contain a subtle signature which can be linked to a person's susceptibility to Type 1 diabetes." Alec Jeffreys, the progenitor of junk DNA fingerprinting, was part of the research team that made the discovery. Jeffreys predicted that "further troubling links between DNA fingerprints and disease will emerge as scientists probe the completed draft of the human genome." One person's "junk" DNA might prove to be another's future wealth of information about genetic conditions.

Finally, we must reckon with the craftiness and adaptability of the criminal mind, which already is trying to outsmart forensic DNA technologies. As *USA Today* recently reported, law enforcement officers in Richmond have found prisoners taking DNA tests for other prisoners, while jailers in Utah have listened in on conversations among prisoners about how to fool the police by planting someone else's blood or semen at the scene of a crime. The most notorious episode to date occurred in Milwaukee, where an inmate intent on undermining the DNA evidence used in his rape conviction had a relative smuggle his semen out of jail in a ketchup packet, then stage a false rape using the sample so that the inmate could argue that he was being set up. After all, how could a man in prison leave DNA evidence at the scene of a crime committed miles away unless he was being framed?

Addressing the Problems

Law enforcement generally characterizes the debate over DNA databases as a choice about how "tough on crime" we wish to be. Discussing proposed legislation to expand the state of Utah's DNA database to include all felons—including those incarcerated, on parole, and on probation—the state representative who helped craft the bill declared: "We're going to protect people. We're going to stop people from getting raped. We're going to stop people from being victimized." Last year [2002], a sheriff in Salt Lake County, Utah, told the local paper, "I would like to take a DNA sample from everyone that gets booked into my jail." Most law enforcement professionals would like to see these DNA databases integrated and linked to databases of criminal history, license plate records, and myriad other public records.

The legal fights about the uses of DNA, both criminal and civilian, are most likely just beginning. In November 2002, for example, a federal judge in Sacramento, California, ruled in favor of Danny Miles, a convicted felon sentenced to probation who refused to provide a DNA sample to his probation officer. The sample was required by the DNA Analysis Backlog Elimination Act, which President Clinton signed into law in 2000. U.S. District Judge William Shubb found persuasive Miles's claim that compulsory DNA sampling violated his Fourth Amendment protections against unreasonable search and seizure.

In addition, the courts have not yet ruled on a far greater problem: the lack of consistent privacy protections for criminal databases and their samples. Currently, the states have a patchwork of protections for their databases, but only a few have thorough regulations for monitoring the privacy of the original samples drawn from the convicted. "Forensic DNA databanks are more highly regulated and protected than any other kind of databanks," Paul Ferrara assured me. "The greater threat to privacy is the ability of unscrupulous people to retrieve others' DNA surreptitiously," as happened recently in a tabloid-style paternity case involving Hollywood producer Steve Bing; a private investigator pilfered his discarded dental floss from the garbage for DNA paternity testing.

But there are serious problems with even these regulated databanks and databases: few have adequate privacy protections; there is no national oversight of the quality of samples or the databases themselves; and there are no consistent regulations regarding who can access information and for what reasons. Implementing three simple practices (all endorsed by the ACLU [American Civil Liberties Union]) would go a long way toward preventing misuse of forensic DNA databases: destruction of the original samples taken; restricting the information stored in the CODIS database to convicted violent felons only; and guarantees that the database would be available to individuals, especially those who did not have access to DNA testing when they were convicted, for purposes of exoneration. But so far, there seems to be no overwhelming public demand for such reforms; most people see DNA fingerprinting as the ultimate crime-fighting tool rather than a potential threat to their liberties. And while there is surely a difference between collecting information on large social groups deemed to be "high-risk" and collecting information on individual criminals and suspects, the rapid expansion of these DNA databases should at least give us pause....

Crossroads Ahead

The creation of new DNA databases and the expansion of existing ones show no signs of slowing. The National Commission on the Future of DNA Evidence (at the National Institute of Justice) projects that . . . the CODIS database will contain the DNA profiles of more than one million felons; by 2010 the commission "expects portable, miniaturized instrumentation that will provide analysis at the crime scene with computer-linked remote analysis." Paralleling these developments in forensic technology will be the increasing knowledge gained by geneticists about DNA markers. "In the future," the Commission concluded, "it is likely that an increasing number of suspects will be identified by database searches."

The resemblance of these new initiatives to crime-fighting schemes of earlier this century is telling. Criminals are often targeted first for the testing of novel social theories. Italian criminologist Cesare Lombroso's theories of hereditary criminal degeneracy prompted compulsory sterilization laws for criminals in several U.S. states in the early twentieth century. Eventually, as eugenic ideas took root in American soil, these compulsory sterilization laws—always billed as progressive measures to protect the public good—expanded to include ever-broader segments of the population.

We complain that our local bank no longer sends us our cancelled checks, and yet we unthinkingly send our DNA out to be banked in perpetuity by strangers.

Researchers are already greedily eyeing the military's DNA database and CODIS as possible resources for locating genetic markers for certain behaviors, including criminal behavior. And it is not difficult to imagine the evolution of a system of criminal profiling based on genetic markers for traits such as aggression, which could then be introduced in criminal prosecutions. In Britain, for example, a recent report by the Nuffield Council on Bioethics suggested that the genetic causes of criminal behavior might eventually be considered as mitigating factors during sentencing of offenders.

Weighing Benefits vs. Risks

As long as genetic samples are voluntary, anonymous, and privacy-protected, the benefits of DNA databases for fighting crime and improving medicine seem to outweigh the risks. At present, however, there is insufficient regulation and oversight of how private companies may use genetic information. Many businesses elide the standards of informed consent with statements that are deliberately misleading, and informed consent is itself an insufficient principle to guide our use of the new genetic technology. Indeed, many of the possible misuses of genetic information are not yet manifest, which makes true consent impossible.

Some of the challenges we face are clearly practical: ensuring the privacy or destruction of original samples; protecting databases from Internet hackers and computer criminals; ensuring access to one's own genetic information or genetic profile if others already possess it. Beyond merely practical concerns, however, it is worth considering what the mining and use of genetic information might mean for how we view ourselves and live our lives. Since the dawn of human reason, we have been intent on classifying the world around us. But the nature and scale of the classification we are now embarking on is altogether different from any we have done before. We live in a world that no longer tolerates the existence of a tomb of the unknowns. We complain that our local bank no longer sends us our cancelled checks, and yet we unthinkingly send our DNA out to be banked in perpetuity by strangers.

Ten years ago, Dorothy Nelkin, a professor at New York University, imagined "a kind of Jonathan Swift scenario—families demanding information about their genetic roots, adoption brokers probing the genetic history of children in order to find appropriate matches, or commercial firms storing genetic profiles and selling them to interested agencies." With the exception of adoption brokers, her predictions have come to pass. Today, information is power, but some information is not unambiguously good for us or others to possess. Not every person will want to know if they carry the gene for a debilitating condition. Not every parent will wish to test their offspring for genetic markers for height, aggression, or sexual orientation. As one writer recently confessed, after being approached by a distant relative to take a DNA test to establish their genealogical link, "It's just that the idea of part of my personal genetic code sitting in some database gives me the creeps."

No Longer Sci-fi

In the 1997 movie *Gattaca*, the main character, a member of the genetic underclass, spends tortured hours figuring out how to outwit the ubiquitous genetic sensors, linked to a universal DNA database, that instantly separate the genetically fit from the unfit. In this brave new society, the genetically weak (or "invalids") are not allowed to pursue certain jobs or romantic interests. Parents turn human procreation over to genetic designers. The society is high-achieving and super-efficient but despotic and stale.

Perhaps such a world seems absurd to us now; our guiding principle is liberty, we tell ourselves, which means allowing individuals to decide for themselves what to do with their genetic information. And yet, step-by-step and often for defensible reasons, we are paving the way for the universal, compulsory, DNA sampling of citizens. These are not simply the musings of science fiction; they are the logical conclusion of the technological infrastructure of DNA identification—such as Britain's Biobank—that we are eagerly building. In the beginning, the reasons for such databases will be familiar, modern, liberal, and compelling: to cure disease, to catch criminals, to ensure that children have a healthy beginning to their lives. But the end in sight is a drastically different society and way of life. We may come to know too much about ourselves to truly live in freedom; and our public and private institutions may know so much about us that equal treatment and personal liberty may become impossible.

We cannot escape our genes—not yet, at least. And we will probably never fully understand the relationship between our biology and our destiny. Human beings will always be at least partially a mystery, and therefore at least partially free. But we can escape or at least limit having our genetic profile spread promiscuously across unregulated, unprotected DNA databases. Participants in the DNA revolution—from forensic DNA database managers to Internet purveyors of paternity tests—are together poised to become one of the most powerful forces for determining the value of our DNA. Before going further down this path, we should pause to consider the benefits and dangers of allowing them to do so.

2

As DNA Databases Grow, the Potential for Abuse and Error Increases

Tania Simoncelli and Helen Wallace

Tania Simoncelli is a science and technology fellow at the American Civil Liberties Union (ACLU). She also is on the board of the Council for Responsible Genetics. Helen Wallace, PhD, is the deputy director of GeneWatch in the UK.

Few persons object to the use of DNA in criminal cases; its value cannot be overstated. But the permanent retention of personal DNA information in some remote database, or worse, the potential for having it misused or shared among remote databases, invokes serious protestation. Setting aside this primary concern, the practical benefits of expanded databases may not trump the social cost. First, they put increasing numbers of innocent persons on "suspect lists" regardless of whether they have ever been convicted of anything, or even charged. The long-term retention of such data (mostly obtained without voluntary consent) is likely to exacerbate discrimination in the form of racial/ethnic or gender profiling. And DNA testing is not infallible. Switched samples, contamination with other DNA, and misinterpretation of DNA analyses are only a few of the dangers that potentially increase as databases grow.

The past decade has witnessed an extraordinary growth in DNA databases for use in criminal intelligence and health

Tania Simoncelli and Helen Wallace, "Spiraling Out of Control," *Index on Censorship*, vol. 34, 2005, pp. 55–60. Reproduced by permission of the publisher, www.indexon line.org.

research. The databases range in size from a few hundred to a few million samples, with the UK [United Kingdom] at the scientific forefront.

The UK's National DNA Database (NDNAD) is the oldest, largest and most inclusive national forensic DNA database in the world. Now in its tenth year of operation [2005], it contains DNA samples and profiles from more than 2.5 million individuals and is expected to expand over the next few years to include some 5 million people, nearly 10 per cent of the population. On file is DNA drawn from a wide range of criminals—from violent offenders to those convicted of misdemeanours by way of others who have eventually been found innocent.

US advances have attempted to keep pace with the UK. Three years after NDNAD went live, the FBI began to operate its own national database and software system: the Combined DNA Index System (CODIS) enables local, state and national authorities to share DNA profiles electronically and contains more than 2.3 million offender DNA profiles. Since 1998, all 50 US states have actively collected DNA from people caught up in the criminal justice system; in 2004, they were connected by CODIS.

Meanwhile, the UK has developed the disturbing tendency to seek samples from an ever-widening range of individuals; it has also decided to collect and permanently retain DNA from people who are merely arrested—and where the UK leads, the US and the rest are following as fast as may be. . . .

Going Global

This expansion is likely to continue. In 2003 alone, 18 US states passed laws to include more categories of people in their databases. In addition, there have been at least two proposals to use DNA samples collected from newborns for medical and law enforcement purposes. In the UK, plans are under way to collect DNA samples from 500,000 adults for medical research and a proposal to collect DNA samples for health purposes from all newborns will be revisited in about five years. Samples in these collections would be linked to National Health Service records, a plausible 'back door' entry for the government should it wish to establish a forensic database.

Meanwhile, DNA databases have gone global. Australia, New Zealand and most European nations have them; China and South Korea have plans to establish them. The government of Portugal recently announced that it would create the world's first universal forensic database and Interpol has gone international with a database that allows all member states to be notified of matches, though it limits access to the profile to the original policing agency.

Implications for Family Members

One controversial use of DNA databases is 'familial searching', which involves looking for 'partial matches' between a crime scene profile and individual profiles on the database. Because close relatives share similar DNA profiles, law enforcement can track down close relatives of individuals identified by a partial match and ask for a DNA sample. First used in the UK in 2002, this method has since been used in at least 20 cases and helped solve five of them. The FBI's director has stated that his organization does not run this type of search. But at least two states, Massachusetts and New York, have regulations that explicitly allow it and most other state laws do not forbid it. So far, we know of no confirmed uses of familial searching in the US, although in one recent case in Kansas it was alleged that the police were led to a suspect by retrieving a DNA sample from the suspect's daughter.

Few people have problems with the use of DNA in criminal cases. The permanent retention of DNA in a database for use in future investigations is, however, another matter. An individual captured in a police database becomes an automatic suspect for all future criminal investigations in which database

searches are used. This undermines the presumption of innocence that is central to many criminal justice systems.

Setting aside this fundamental problem, benefits of the use
and expansion of these databases must be weighed against
their social costs: while the temptation on the part of law enforcement is to put more people into the database, the practical benefits of expansion may be limited. In the UK, for example, despite the large number of people on the database,
DNA profiles are obtained from the examination of less than
1 per cent of crime scenes. In 2002 and 2003, only 1.6 per
cent of all crime detections were attributed to DNA database
matches, including only 0.3 per cent of all detections for violent and sexual offences.

At the same time, there are many reasons to be concerned
about the use and expansion of police databases, including
their impact on individual privacy, their potential for misuse
by governments, discrimination and the possibility of error
and wrongful conviction.

The Debate over Sample Retention

Unlike a fingerprint, DNA has the potential to provide information about health and relationships, including one's risk of
having or developing a genetic condition. Many concerns
about DNA collections stem from the permanent retention of
the biological sample—a practice that is common to both UK
and US databanks. The DNA *profiles* held on the database are
usually sufficient for identifying a person and his/her relatives.
They are unlikely to contain personal genetic information
about health or other characteristics. DNA *samples*, however,
contain virtually unlimited amounts of genetic information.
In the UK, all DNA samples are currently retained indefinitely,
linked to an individual's record on the database. In the US,
samples can also be retained indefinitely, although some states
require authorities to expunge DNA records upon reversals or
convictions.

Law enforcement authorities in both countries have argued that sample retention is necessary for 'quality assurance purposes'. But re-testing the same sample clearly cannot correct many errors, including sample mix-ups. In fact, in both the UK and the US, testing of a fresh DNA sample from the suspect is always required before the DNA evidence is admissible. The UK government's advisory body, the Human Genetics Commission, has concluded that the reasons given for retaining samples are 'not compelling'; although the UK Home Office recognises that the retention of DNA samples is 'one of the most sensitive issues to the wider public', it currently has no plans to change this practice.

Because DNA samples are collected without consent, genetic research using the samples and/or database bypasses the usual safeguards, such as the need for informed consent from participants and review by an ethics committee.

Potential for Misuse

The potential for misuse of stored DNA samples is real. It can reveal personal genetic or family information, or be wrongly acquired for controversial genetic research. Moreover, threats to genetic privacy extend well beyond the millions of people whose samples are currently on file because of the family overlap. Genetic research using the database is likely to be misleading as well as controversial.

In the UK, uses of the database are limited to crime detection and prevention but include controversial research such as attempts to predict ethnicity from DNA profiles. Because DNA samples are collected without consent, genetic research using the samples and/or database bypasses the usual safeguards, such as the need for informed consent from participants and review by an ethics committee. Categories in the NDNAD such as 'ethnic appearance'—as determined by a police officer—are meaningless for scientific purposes and the DNA profiles and samples will not be representative of either the general or 'criminal' population.

Thirteen US state laws include a vague, open-ended authorization allowing the database to be used for 'other humanitarian purposes'; Alabama, for instance, explicitly authorizes the creation and use of a DNA population statistical database 'to provide data relative to the causation, detection and prevention of disease or disability' as well as to assist in educational or medical research.

The use of 'familial searching' raises an additional privacy concern since it risks revealing cases of non-paternity or other relationships that may be unknown to the members of a suspect's family.

The dramatic expansion of UK and US databases, particularly the process of including people who have merely been arrested, has redefined the nature and purpose of these so-called 'criminal' databases. Because DNA is such a powerful tool in tracing individuals, law enforcement databases could well be used as instruments of government surveillance.

The UK database now contains the first permanent list of those arrested since April 2004 along with their DNA samples and profiles. In the US, California's new law means that this year more than 600,000 people will qualify for testing, a tenfold increase. From 2009, all of California's 425,000 annual felony arrests will qualify for testing; yet 60 per cent of these will ultimately not be convicted of any crime. Profiles from all those arrested and charged will also be uploaded into CODIS, even if they are eventually proved innocent. California will also retain suspect DNA—including that which is voluntarily provided during 'DNA dragnets' or 'mass screenings'—for up to two years. These DNA profiles can be 'speculatively searched' for matches with DNA profiles from any number of investigations.

Everyone Is a Suspect

Expanding the databases puts an increasing number of unsuspecting people on a 'suspect list' regardless of whether they have ever been charged or convicted. This may subtly alter the way they are viewed both by the state and by their fellow citizens, potentially undermining the principles of 'innocent until proved guilty' and of rehabilitation. Without adequate protections, permanent records of arrest could be used to restrict people's rights and freedoms, making it difficult or impossible for them to obtain travel visas or employment.

Miscarriages of justice this far should caution us against too great a reliance on the wonders of the DNA database.

Life-long retention of data is also likely to exacerbate discrimination against certain groups of people, particularly ethnic minorities. Racial bias permeates society and the criminal justice systems in both the UK and US. A study in California in the early 1990s revealed that an astonishing 92 per cent of the black men arrested by police on drug charges were subsequently released for lack of evidence or inadmissible evidence. In the UK, *New Scientist* magazine calculated that the DNA database now contains DNA profiles from nearly one third of black adult males, compared to only 8 per cent of white adult men.

Within living memory, both fascist and communist governments in Europe have used identity papers and personal records to oppress particular sectors of their populations. In the US, census records were used during World War II to round up and intern innocent Japanese-Americans. Since [the terrorist attacks of] 11 September, 2001, many people of Arabic, Middle Eastern or South Asian descent have been detained, arrested or harassed by government authorities. Some forensic scientists argue that the only way to prevent discrimination is to expand DNA databases to include whole populations.

Not that this will end discrimination generally, as recent attempts to use crime scene samples to predict the genetic ancestry of potential suspects indicates. Results for ancestry might be misleading and the genetics of predicting eye, skin or hair colour is extremely complex and poorly understood; the police might misinterpret the information they are given. Without better oversight, there is a danger that such tests will be used selectively to reinforce existing prejudices.

Despite what the media chooses to portray, DNA testing is not infallible. DNA samples can be switched or contaminated; analyses can be misinterpreted, especially when crime scene samples contain mixtures of DNA from more than one source or where DNA is degraded; and results can be mistakenly reported.

The fallibility of DNA testing was made painfully clear when, in January 2003, the Houston, Texas Police Department's crime lab was shut down following an investigation that revealed widespread problems including gross mishandling and misinterpretation of DNA evidence by laboratory personnel. Some 1,300 cases are under review and, to date, one person, Josiah Sutton, has been released from prison after serving four years for a crime he did not commit. Errors are likely to multiply as databases expand, becoming the rule rather than the exception. Miscarriages of justice this far should caution us against too great a reliance on the wonders of the DNA database.

3

Expanding The Categories in DNA Databases Will Solve More Crimes

Steve Chapman

Steve Chapman is a columnist with the Chicago Tribune *and a frequent contributor to RealClearPolitics.com.*

Had DNA databases been expanded years ago to include suspects and arrestees and not just convicted felons, many persons ultimately murdered would still be alive. DNA is to the twenty-first century what fingerprints were to the twentieth century. It should therefore be used just as extensively. The broader the database, the more crimes will be prevented as well as solved.

During the 1990s, a vicious criminal was preying on women on the South Side of Chicago. The first victim was found beaten to death in a vacant lot in 1993. Police found DNA evidence at the scene. They found DNA evidence from the same assailant in seven other murders and a rape. But they couldn't match it to anyone.

Finally, in 2000, police arrested a man who had been seen with two of the victims shortly before they died. Andre Crawford confessed, a DNA analysis implicated him, and he was ultimately charged with killing 11 women.

You could interpret that outcome as a great success for our use of DNA technology in law enforcement. Or you could interpret it as a huge, tragic failure.

Steve Chapman, "Fighting Crime With One Hand Behind Our Backs," RealClearPolitics .com, October 9, 2005. Reproduced by permission of Steve Chapman and Creators Syndicate, Inc.

Between 1993 and 2000, the years encompassing his alleged spree of rape and murder, Crawford was arrested four times. But Illinois law allows police to take DNA samples only from suspects who have been convicted. So his genetic profile never showed up in the state database, where it could have been matched to that of the killer.

Had it been taken when Crawford was picked up for felony theft in 1993, he could have been stopped after the first murder. Ten women who are now dead might be alive today.

A Valuable Tool

DNA is one of the most valuable and reliable tools ever conceived for law enforcement and criminal justice. It has been used to solve a wide array of crimes that otherwise would have gone unpunished, and it has freed hundreds of people who were mistakenly convicted and even sent to death row. It offers vast benefits in preventing crime. But we have yet to take the obvious step to realize its potential.

The bigger the database, the more crimes will be solved, the more crimes will be prevented, and the more innocent lives will be spared.

As a rule, police fingerprint everyone they arrest. Those prints are kept on file, where they can be matched against those found at crime scenes. But when it comes to DNA, the cops are fighting crime with one hand tied behind their backs. The prevailing practice across the country is to take DNA samples only from people convicted of felonies. That greatly limits the number of samples in state and federal DNA databases that can yield hits.

But the U.S. Senate wants to change that policy as far as the federal government is concerned. Recently it approved a measure that would mandate the collection of DNA samples from everyone arrested or detained by federal agents, and would allow some states to submit samples from their arrestees. DNA is to the 21st century what fingerprints were to the 20th. So why shouldn't it be used just as extensively?

Californians have already answered that question by saying, "No reason at all." Last year, they approved a ballot initiative requiring the collection of DNA samples from anyone convicted of a felony or certain other offenses. Starting in 2009, under the new law, every adult who is merely arrested for a felony will have to surrender his DNA.

Some civil liberties groups oppose these changes because DNA, unlike fingerprints, contains a wealth of personal information that might be misused by the government. That's not a trivial concern. But laws already contain strict provisions to assure that DNA can be used only to identify criminals.

Critics also think it's unfair to keep the DNA of people who may be innocent. But the unfairness is minimal. You don't suffer any injury from having your genetic information on file with the cops—unless you decide to commit a crime.

More Samples, Less Crime

In any case, the small risk of abuse has to be weighed against the huge potential benefits. The bigger the database, the more crimes will be solved, the more crimes will be prevented, and the more innocent lives will be spared.

British police now are allowed to take swabs from anyone arrested for a crime carrying a prison sentence. As a result, they now have 2.5 million genetic profiles, which is the largest in the world as a share of its population. Our national database, by contrast, has only 2.7 million samples—even though our population is nearly five times larger than Britain's.

The result is that the British catch a lot more criminals than we do. The FBI system has gotten 16,309 hits since it began operating seven years ago. The British get 50,000 matches *a year*.

In recent years, DNA has shown its enormous worth in exonerating the innocent. Now we need to put it to full use catching the guilty.

4

Expanding DNA Databases Beyond Convictees Is Unjust

National Association of Criminal Defense Lawyers (NACDL)

The National Association of Criminal Defense Lawyers (NACDL), with approximately thirteen thousand members nationwide, is the preeminent professional bar association representing U.S. criminal defense professionals. The organization provides policy and position statements and/or legal amicus briefs (arguments submitted for the court's consideration by persons or entities who are not parties to the litigation, but who have a strong interest or concern in the subject matter at issue) for use in motions and appellate briefs in federal and state courts.

DNA databases clearly have the potential to improve the nation's criminal justice system. However, expanding the databases to include DNA samples of persons not convicted of any serious crime—for example, mere arrestees who are later proved innocent, juvenile offenders, or innocent persons caught in DNA dragnets—creates its own harms. These include distorted reflection of racially disparate arrest rates, compromise of confidential juvenile proceedings, and the potential abuse of very private information regarding physical traits and/or genetic conditions. DNA databanks should be limited in scope to convictees of serious crimes, and state/federal authorities should carry the burden to expunge DNA records of all others.

National Association of Criminal Defense Lawyers (NACDL), "Resolution of the NACDL Board of Directors Regarding the Expansion of DNA Databases," nacdl.org, February 21, 2004. Reproduced by permission.

D NA databases have the potential to improve the fairness and accuracy of our criminal justice system by excluding innocent suspects, exonerating the wrongly convicted and identifying the true guilty parties.

The Federal government and all 50 states and the District of Columbia have laws requiring the collection of DNA samples for criminal investigation purposes, and these laws have increasingly been amended to expand the categories of individuals from whom samples are required.

DNA database laws once limited in scope to serious sex offenders are now being expanded to include all felonies, mis-demeanors, arrestees, and juvenile offenders.

Revealing Private Information

DNA samples can reveal extremely sensitive, private informa-tion regarding physical and mental traits and the likelihood of the occurrence of genetic conditions and diseases, and, as Jus-tice Brennan wrote in his concurrence in *Whalen v. Roe*, "The central storage and easy accessibility of computerized data vastly increase the potential for abuse of that information".

Too many DNA database systems place the burden of ex-punging records on individuals who have been exoner-ated of crimes instead of the state, which falsely accused them in the first place.

Expanding DNA databases to include profiles from arrest-ees will produce an identification system that reflects and pos-sibly exacerbates racially disparate arrest rates, in part because the inclusion of arrestees provides an incentive for pretext and race-based arrests for the purpose of DNA sampling.

The U.S. National Commission on the Future of DNA Evi-dence, in 2002, recommended against including samples from arrestees on the ground that there were already hundreds of thousands of samples waiting to be analyzed and state crime laboratories do not have the capacity to process more samples.

Burdening the Innocent

Experience with DNA dragnets in which large numbers of individuals in a geographic area are asked to provide samples, sometimes based on racial descriptions, demonstrates that this law enforcement technique subjects innocent persons to intimidation and harassment by law enforcement officials.

Confidentiality and the practice of expunging records are essential to the juvenile justice system's principal goals of treatment and rehabilitation, and policies which undermine the confidentiality of juvenile proceedings distort this rehabilitative model and threaten to stigmatize juvenile offenders.

Too many DNA database systems place the burden of expunging records on individuals who have been exonerated of crimes instead of the state, which falsely accused them in the first place.

No to Expansion

The National Association of Criminal Defense Lawyers opposes the creation of a population-wide DNA database and the use of DNA dragnets;

The National Association of Criminal Defense Lawyers opposes the expansion of DNA database laws to require inclusion of DNA profiles from individuals convicted of misdemeanors, juvenile offenders, and arrestees.

The National Association of Criminal Defense Lawyers supports legislation that requires state and federal authorities to automatically expunge DNA profiles from individuals whose convictions are overturned on appeal or through postconviction proceedings or other mechanisms.

5

Physical Profiles in DNA Databases Narrow the Scope of Potential Suspects

Lindsy A. Elkins

Lindsy A. Elkins practices law with the Illinois firm of Swanson, Martin & Bell, LLP. She received her law degree from Notre Dame Law School, where she is a teaching assistant for Notre Dame Law School's Writing Program, and article director for the Notre Dame Journal of Law, Ethics, & Public Policy.

Scientific analysis of DNA material includes the ability to determine gender, height, eye color, race, and ethnicity from the examined sample. Such information allows law enforcement professionals to accelerate their search by focusing on a more narrow pool of potential suspects. It also allows attorneys to avoid statute of limitation problems by obtaining "John Doe" DNA warrants that indict yet-unnamed defendants. Privacy concerns are defeated by the fact that law enforcement personnel have long used racial and other classifications to narrow their searches; DNA samples merely render those searches more precise. Moreover, the use of race or other personal traits to identify a particular perpetrator does not disadvantage any particular group; therefore, such profiling will generally survive equal protection challenges. Ultimately, an understanding of the relationship between genetics and criminal behavior can assist in the development of more effective criminal justice laws and policies.

Lindsy A. Elkins, "Five Foot Two with Eyes of Blue: Physical Profiling and the Prospect of a Genetics-Based Criminal Justice System," *Notre Dame Journal of Law, Ethics, & Public Policy*, vol. 17, 2003, pp. 269–305. Copyright © 2003 by Thomas J. White Center on Law & Government. Reproduced by permission.

Scientists now have the ability to identify an indefinite number of physical traits including height, eye color, sex, and race from a trace of DNA material. Recent breakthroughs in the Human Genome Project (HGP) mandate an expansion of DNA evidence as an investigative tool.

The HGP began in 1986 in the Department of Energy as an effort to systematically sequence and decode all the information in the entire human genome. It is the "most extensively funded national science program since the Apollo space mission." The primary goal is to pinpoint all 140,000 genes on twenty-three pairs of chromosomes and to sequence all of the 3.5 billion DNA units that make up the pairs. The project will serve as a reference for the entire scientific community. Scientists have already completed a working draft in the year 2000 that allows for identification of most of the genes in our genome [The HGP was completed in 2003. It found that humans have fewer genes than had been expected.]. . .

This foundational work allows researchers to accelerate studies to characterize these genes and determine their functions. The technology will revolutionize the way our criminal justice system handles cases both with and without suspects as well as unidentified victims in which a sample of their DNA is available. . . .

Arguments against DNA have . . . shifted from reliability and certainty issues to broader concerns for privacy. Opponents have condemned the use of DNA as a threat to "the constitutional guarantee of a fair trial" [Mark Hansen]. The major moral concern about DNA use for identification purposes is not whether the DNA is a piece or property of the person identified or whether it was extracted by force from the person. "Civil libertarians . . . fear that the information contained in DNA databanks could be used for purposes other than criminal identification, such as trying to determine whether an individual is genetically predisposed to certain kinds of behaviors" [Hansen]. It is the individual's informational privacy, what DNA can disclose about the identified person, that is the basis of concern. The debate is thus framed around informational privacy as a policy challenge: What should society be allowed to learn about its citizens in the course of attempting to identify them? In order to answer this question, the informational nature of DNA must be examined.

Including such physical trait markers or "population specific alleles" (PSAs) in databanks and criminal investigations would support open case file systems that would take advantage of additional information to narrow the search for the suspect or sample source.

Use by Prosecutors

Many jurisdictions are incorporating these breakthroughs into powerful new law enforcement tools. The power of science is affecting cases nationwide. Prosecutors are now using DNA to circumvent legal barriers. Attorneys are basing indictments solely on the DNA profiles of yet unidentified suspects. The indictments, called John Doe or DNA warrants, provide [according to Michael Luo] "no name, as would normally accompany the charges, instead listing a series of letters and numbers designating certain measurements of DNA segments that, taken together, represent the rapist's unique DNA profile." This method prevents the statute of limitations from running out on rape cases. [All states and the federal government limit the time in which a case may be brought against a person.] The warrants also allow police a means to continue the pursuit of suspects who leave behind DNA evidence. Finally, the warrants also help to combat the nationwide problem of backlogs of untested DNA samples that remain in evidence lockers because crime labs are too overwhelmed to examine them. . . .

Including the genetic profile in the indictment is helpful to circumvent legal barriers like statutes of limitation. However, it does not aid in the actual identification match with a suspect. Traditionally, law enforcement officers sought eyewitness testimony to obtain physical descriptions as a method to facilitate crime solving. However, eyewitness descriptions are often unreliable or there may be no eyewitnesses to a crime in the first place. Virtually all jurisdictions around the country have open case file samples from crime scenes, battlefields, or plane crash sites that are yet unidentified. Two decades ago, the best known current humanitarian use of DNA, identification of remains at the World Trade Center, would have been unimaginable.

The Ultimate Identifier

In reference to these collections of unidentified samples, investigators will want to glean as much information as possible about the person through DNA analysis so that they can profile their missing sample source. [According to Hugh Miller], scientists can now discern from DNA "a virtually indefinite number of physical traits possessed by an individual, from height, eye color, sex, and race, down to the shapes of a person's toes." "In addition, genetic typing permits inferences as to inherited disorders and may offer clues to facial or other bodily features." [Edward J. Imwinkelried and D.H. Kaye]. Thus, a DNA profile in the databank that matches that from a crime scene is more useful than traditional composite sketching and "may act as the ultimate eyewitness or ultimate profiler" [Michelle Hibbert]. "Genetically-derived trait information may be superior to human-derived trait information" because "[u]nlike humans, machines often cannot be fooled by changes in physical appearance" [Hibbert]. Furthermore, it is not yet possible to alter one's genetic makeup; thus, physical changes are unlikely to conceal a suspect.

Including such physical trait markers or "population specific alleles" (PSAs) in databanks and criminal investigations would support open case file systems that would take advantage of additional information to narrow the search for the suspect or sample source. This would also "take the guesswork out of deciding against which racial reference group to assess a particular sample" [Eric T. Juengst]. Profiling DNA samples for racial or ethnic characteristics, however, is a hotly contested proposition. . . . Scientists disagree over dividing the U.S. population into sub-populations for statistical purposes. Some argue detailed genetic variation studies of the population along ethnic and geographic lines are required. Others argue that logistical difficulties outweigh the minimal statistical benefits of extensively subdividing the population for forensic purposes.

Ethnicity and Race

Despite the disagreement, "it is [currently] possible to identify a collection of genetic markers that are distinctive enough to allow confident genetic [ethnic affiliation estimation]" [Juengst]. It is also feasible to identify and estimate individual interethnic characteristics within first or second generation hybrids of one or more populations. Investigators do this by markers called "population specific alleles" (PSAs), marking the ethnic populations that are our traditional races like European Americans, African Americans, Native Americans, and Asian Americans. In the United States, the mixture of populations and hybridization has obscured genetic differences among the resident populations. However, when scientists "focus on the small amount of difference between populations, a distinct pattern of genetic variation among populations emerges, with Sub-Saharan African populations having the most genetic variations, European and South West Asian populations less, East Asian populations still less, and Amerindian populations the least" [Kenneth K. Kidd]. Thus, technicians can now include ethnic affiliation in the profile of the sample. . . .

Despite current genetic findings dispelling the myth of any biological races, opponents find the inclusion of ethnic geographic markers problematic. . . . It threatens a move from using social categories to classify the markers to using the markers to classify our social categories. . . .

Genetic trait profiling can pass constitutional muster under the Fourth Amendment, which addresses the constitutionality of police stops, detentions, and arrests, because it is not officer-initiated.

Finally, opponents argue that inclusion of these markers would increase privacy concerns beyond that of traditional fingerprinting by reporting the socially sensitive racial classification of an arrestee. This argument fails to recognize that law enforcement officers have long used racial classifications. Mug shot photographs, for example, reveal race or ethnicity by showing superficial distinctions that we use to socially categorize. Opponents also argue that this process could reveal family ancestral secrets, thus causing a suspect psychological or social harm by upsetting her social identity. Furthermore, the information revealed is not unique only to the donor, but also reveals the private concerns of the donor's parents, children, and siblings. This information increases the potential power to stigmatize and discriminate against many subjects. Our country is already sour on the notion of "low tech" racial profiling in law enforcement. Some contend that using genetic markers to limit investigations to suspects of a single social "race" would be vulnerable to an equal protection claim. . . .

Constitutional Challenge

Genetic trait profiling can pass constitutional muster under the Fourth Amendment, which addresses the constitutionality of police stops, detentions, and arrests, because it is not officer-initiated. Under Fourth Amendment analysis, an officer's motive "does not make otherwise lawful conduct illegal or unconstitutional" [*Whren v. United States*]. Racial profiling implies a requisite degree of mental intent or discriminatory purpose. When race is used merely as an element in the description of a particular perpetrator no probabilistic problems occur. The proposition that more congruent details increase the likelihood of identity between suspect and perpetrator seems indisputable. . . .

Police investigations have long used race as an identifying characteristic. "Law enforcement officers [nationwide] routinely treat race as a prominent component of a suspect description, investigating only individuals of the same race as the assailant" [R. Richard Banks]. . . . Genetically-derived physical profiles will function in the same manner, except that DNA will become the eye-witness. Thus, the physical profiles should survive an equal protection challenge because no group is singled out for special treatment and no one is penalized because of hostility toward a particular trait or race. . . .

The rationale for expanding database categories is that violent criminals often commit lesser crimes first, thus the sooner their DNA is in a database, the more likely they will be caught first.

Use of genetically derived traits could lead to the apprehension of more criminals from one race than another—but not because of official hostility toward particular races or individuals' prejudices about those races. By using DNA samples from crime scenes, statistically valid inferences as to race cannot lead the authorities to target minorities because there would be no opportunity to draw from subjective racial stereotypes or prejudices. . . . If DNA analysis indicated that the source of a sample was more likely to be Caucasian than

African-American, it might help overcome a stereotypical assumption that officers need only consider blacks as prime suspects. The genetic description will constrain police officers' selection of suspects and might thereby serve as a check on improper state motives or bias. . . . It could also serve to exonerate those wrongly accused or incarcerated. Furthermore, it may eliminate the initial reliance on stereotypes and outdated low-tech profiles in the search for a suspect by defining the characteristics of the suspect.

Databases

In order to maximize the effectiveness of identification in a case with an unidentified suspect, the subsequent profile generated by the lab should also be included in and matched against existing DNA databases after a physical profile is derived. All fifty states have passed laws setting up crime fighting DNA databases over the last 13 years. . . .

The national trend is to include more individuals and expand databases. . . . The rationale for expanding database categories is that violent criminals often commit lesser crimes first, thus the sooner their DNA is in a database, the more likely they will be caught first. . . .

Compelling statistics also prove that these databases have the power to exonerate suspects already serving time for a crime they did not commit. Constitutionally, the databases have the support of the precedent of computerized fingerprint databases. Furthermore, the courts have upheld recent efforts to expand included criminal classes. . . . Our criminal justice system has only just begun to realize the benefits of database use. . . .

Inherited Traits

Studies clearly show that heredity and genetics make a significant contribution to the development of antisocial or criminal behavior. In an effort to pinpoint the specific origins of deviant behavior, researchers have attempted to identify relevant physiological processes and corresponding dysfunctions. Studies have been conducted across fields such as neurology, psychophysiology, and endocrinology. "Although the results have not yet provided conclusive evidence of clear and direct biological 'causes' of crime, considerable data has emerged to support the argument that genetics have a real and significant influence on the development and expression of human behavior" [Maureen P. Coffey].

Nevertheless, scientists also recognize that criminality is a complex behavior involving the interaction of multiple risk factors. People do not possess a single gene for crime. Many studies purporting to demonstrate the genetic components of behavioral traits do not yet warrant the publicity accorded to them in the media. Although the gene mapping studies are becoming quite sophisticated, there is no convincing evidence yet for direct linkage of genes to human behaviors. Because of the success in this area of study demonstrating the genetic components of behavioral traits, society should be ready to accurately interpret the implications of such a find. . . .

Currently, a person's genetically ingrained traits, mental or physical, can be seen as a set of parameters that fix a background space of possibilities within which the person is free to create a unique character of his own free will. [As Hugh Miller noted in *DNA Blueprints, Personhood, and Genetic Privacy*]

> Recent and impending advances in genetic science do not necessitate any transformation in our concept of personal identity or character into essentially genetic terms. Genetic traits, be they mental or physical in nature, are simply the raw material from which an individual creates a unique character through the operation of his own autonomous will.

6

Using DNA Databases for Targeted Profiling Is Ineffective

Samuel Walker

Professor Samuel Walker teaches criminal justice at the University of Nebraska at Omaha.

DNA dragnets or "sweeps" are searches in which police ask individuals to give voluntary DNA samples in an effort to identify a perpetrator of a crime or series of crimes. The dragnets may be broad sweeps of all persons in an area, or may be limited to specific DNA profiles matching those of the suspect/perpetrator, e.g., by race, gender, etc. A national survey of all reported cases in which police requested voluntary DNA samples from potential suspects found that such DNA dragnets resulted in the identification of an offender in only one of the 18 examined cases. Some of the dragnets involved samples from as many as 1,200 to 2,300 persons. In the only case that resulted in a match, the sweep involved DNA testing of only 25 persons. Based on these findings, law enforcement agencies should not conduct DNA sweeps until better model policies are developed that are more narrowly tailored to achieve the intended result (a match), and that better address the collection and handling of DNA evidence.

The use of genetic DNA evidence in the investigation of crimes has had a significant impact on the criminal justice system. Today, all 50 states have some form of mandatory DNA testing for convicted offenders. DNA evidence left at the

Samuel Walker, "Police DNA 'Sweeps' Extremely Unproductive," www.policeaccountability.org/dnareport.pdf, September 2004. Reproduced by permission.

scene of a crime is often used to identify suspects by attempting to match their profile with those already on file in state and national databases. There have been many cases across the country where persons convicted of a crime and sentenced to prison have subsequently been exonerated on the basis of DNA evidence.

In response to the potential uses of DNA evidence in the criminal justice system, the National Institute of Justice created the National Commission on the Future of DNA Evidence in 1998 and has published two reports on DNA testing. Also, the National Research Council has published two reports on the subject.

Fishing with a Net

When law enforcement investigators have little information to go on in the investigation of violent crimes, they sometimes resort to DNA evidence. When the query of existing databases fails to offer a suspect, law enforcement sometimes employ the use of a DNA "sweep" or "dragnet." These searches involve the collection and analysis of DNA from individuals who fit a general description or profile of the suspected offender. Controversies have arisen in several communities when those profiles are extremely vague, with the result that hundreds or even thousands of innocent persons are asked to give DNA samples. There has been virtually no discussion of this aspect of DNA testing and there are presently no model policies to guide law enforcement agencies in requesting voluntary DNA samples from citizens.

A DNA "sweep" is defined as a situation where the police ask a number of individuals to give voluntary DNA samples in an effort to identify the perpetrator of a crime or series of crimes.

Questionable Efficacy

The issue of DNA sweeps arose in Omaha, Nebraska in June of 2004, when the Omaha Police Department began a DNA dragnet in search of a serial rapist responsible for the sexual assault of four women in the last two years. Information received as part of the investigation has the Omaha Police focused on African-American employees of the Omaha Public Power District (OPPD). That list of possible suspects was reportedly narrowed to a list of about 36 men.

The Omaha controversy led to this study of similar DNA sweeps in the United States. The purpose of the study was to determine how often DNA sweeps are used and how successful they are in identifying criminal offenders. The study found that since 1990, there have been eighteen reported sweeps in the United States including the Omaha search. There may have been other cases that were not reported in the news media or were not traceable through conventional web search techniques.

This study does not address the legal issues surrounding DNA sweeps. It covers *only* cases where the police requested DNA samples in an effort to identify an offender. It does *not* cover cases where DNA was used as evidence against a suspect who was already in custody. It also did not cover cases where DNA was used to exonerate a previously convicted person.

It is not known exactly how many DNA sweeps have actually occurred.

The information on DNA sweeps was gathered using traditional Internet search engines. Key words used were "DNA dragnet," "DNA sweeps," and "DNA swabs." Subsequent to the internet search, a more comprehensive search of news articles was completed through the use of the Lexis-Nexis database at the University of Nebraska-Omaha library. The web sites www.dnaresource.com and of the Innocence Project (www.innocenceproject.com) which publish DNA-related news were also searched.

Disappointing Results

DNA sweeps produced a suspected offender in only one of the eighteen cases examined. This suggests that DNA sweeps are extremely unproductive in identifying criminal suspects.

Because they are highly unproductive, possibly unconstitutional, and often aggravate racial tensions, it is recommended that law enforcement agencies not conduct DNA sweeps based on general descriptions or profiles of subjects.

The one case where a criminal suspect was identified involved one of the fewest number of persons asked to give a DNA sample. This case in Lawrence, Massachusetts, involved the sexual assault of a nursing home resident. Consequently, the police began with a short list of potential suspects based on employment and access to the victim.

Several of the cases involved an extremely large number of persons asked to give DNA samples. A 1994 case in Miami, Florida, involved samples from 2,300 people. A 2002 case from Baton Rouge, Louisiana, involved 1,200 people. A 1990 case in San Diego involved over 800 people.

It is not known exactly how many DNA sweeps have actually occurred. Some of the cases listed here were not originally identified through the basic search techniques used but were reported to the authors of this report by knowledgeable individuals. The survey also found references in media accounts to additional cases that could not be independently confirmed.

Scant Results Cannot Justify DNA Sweeps

The evidence suggests that DNA sweeps are extremely unproductive as an investigative technique. A suspect was identified through a DNA sweep in only one of the eighteen reported cases. DNA sweeps also generate controversies over racial profiling and possible violations of constitutional law.

Because they are highly unproductive, possibly unconstitutional, and often aggravate racial tensions, *it is recommended that law enforcement agencies not conduct DNA sweeps based on general descriptions or profiles of suspects.*

Because advances in DNA technology are creating new opportunities for identifying criminal suspects and exonerating convicted offenders, *it is recommended that the law enforcement profession, in consultation with community groups and legal experts, develop a model policy and procedures to guide agencies in the collection and use of DNA evidence.*

The National Institute of Justice (1999) published a brochure, *What Every Law Enforcement Officer Should Know About DNA Evidence,* but it contains no guidance regarding the conduct of DNA sweeps. Similarly, the two reports published by the National Research Council Press do not discuss the potential abuses in DNA sweeps. The 1992 report, *DNA Technology in Forensic Science* devotes one and a half pages (out of 176) to "Abuse and Misuse of DNA Information" but with no mention of sweeps. In testimony before the National Commission on the Future of DNA Evidence, Barry Steinhardt of the ACLU was perhaps the only person to raise questions about the dangers of DNA sweeps by the police.

Some More Promising Uses

It is important to understand the role that DNA plays in different stages of the criminal justice system. While DNA evidence has proven to be extremely valuable in some stages of the system, this report indicates that attempts to use it in another stage is highly problematic. There are three basic stages of the criminal justice system where DNA evidence has been used: pre-arrest investigations; post-arrest-investigations; post-conviction investigations. The web site of the Innocence Project (www.innocenceproject.org) has a wealth of information on the use of DNA in exonerating falsely convicted persons. . . .

Aggravating the problems related to DNA sweeps is that the success of DNA evidence in post-arrest or post-conviction situations has led some people to believe that it can be equally successful in all stages of the criminal justice system. This report clearly indicates to the contrary that pre-arrest DNA sweeps are highly unproductive. In his testimony before the National Commission on the Future of DNA Evidence in 1999, Barry Steinhardt of the ACLU [American Civil Liberties Union] characterized the process of extending a policy or procedure from one purpose (where it is presumptively valid) to another (where it may not be) as "function creep."

Further aggravating the problem is that all of the cases reported so far involve murder and/or rape. Three involved multiple murders and nine involved more than one rape (usually described as "serial rape"). These particularly vicious crimes generate fear among citizens and put pressure on the police to identify and arrest the perpetrator. The result has been the use of a technique that is both highly unproductive and which violates individual constitutional rights.

7

DNA Databases Can Help Assess Damages in Personal Injury Litigation

Jordan K. Garrison

Jordan K. Garrison received her juris doctorate in 2004 from the University of Texas School of Law.

Following the successful sequencing of the human genome under the Human Genome Project, continued research of compiled DNA data has led to the correlation of defective genes with specific diseases and medical conditions. Previously, DNA database information had been used primarily for identifying specific individuals, but now it can be used for its predictive value in exposing latent or potential illness, disease, or other genetic variation in specific individuals. Courts have embraced DNA evidence in criminal proceedings and paternity disputes, but the civil court system has been more reluctant to allow discovery or admissibility of DNA's predictive capabilities. However, such evidence should be allowed when directly relevant to the issues in contention, and may help plaintiffs as well as defendants in assessing the true value of alleged physical harm or injury.

A new day is upon us, here in the age of the genetic revolution. With the completion of the Human Genome Project and continuing research, defects in certain areas of the genome have been correlated to specific diseases with varying degrees of accuracy and specificity. Some areas of the law,

Jordan K. Garrison, "Courts Face the Exciting and the Inevitable: DNA in Civil Trials," *Review of Litigation*, vol. 23, spring 2004, pp. 435–461 (AN 12874123). Reproduced by permission.

such as criminal and paternity cases, already utilize the type of information that genetic evidence can provide. The civil-court system, however, has been much more fearful of allowing the discovery or admissibility of genetic evidence in tort cases [civil lawsuits involving wrongful conduct that causes injury or harm, and for which the law recognizes a remedy]. . . .

Because DNA is a reliable predictor for some types of illnesses and will continue to become a more accurate tool, the tort system must embrace genetic evidence as a new way to bring fairness into the courtroom. . . .

Predicting and Identifying Through DNA

Single defective genes cause thousands of known diseases, such as cystic fibrosis [a congenital disease involving mucus glands], muscular dystrophies [a chronic disease of muscle deterioration], and retinitis pigmentosa [inflammatory disease involving the light-sensitive membrane of the eye]. Because these genes are inherited according to the classic laws of Mendelian genetic [the principal laws of heredity, formulated by Gregor Mendel], their inheritance is predictable. In cases of monogenic diseases [regulated by one gene], the gene will manifest itself in its possessor regardless of environmental factors. People with a presymptomatic genetic condition [one that exists prior to exhibiting symptoms] will develop the disease if they live long enough.

Genetic information does not differ sufficiently from other health-related information to warrant special protection.

In addition to being predictive in nature, genetic information also can be an identifier. DNA fingerprinting is now available to analyze the nucleotide [organic compound] sequences of a bodily source, such as hair, blood, or semen, in order to determine an individual's unique genetic profile. . . .

Courts use the identifying characteristics of DNA, but they do not yet fully embrace its possible predictive qualities. Both paternity and criminal cases routinely use genetic evidence to establish the truth. . . .

With regard to how the court system currently deals with genetic information in civil cases, outside of paternity matters, very little case law exists. In fact, no case exists in which courts have ordered genetic testing to aid in a determination of lifetime-expectancy damages. Courts have compelled genetic testing in a few unreported cases, but in these cases, the courts failed to articulate their reasons. . . .

No Special Protection

Recently, the Task Force on Genetic Information and Insurance of the NIH-DOE [National Institutes of Health/U.S. Department of Energy] Joint Working Group on the Ethical, Legal, and Social Implications of the Human Genome Project decided that genetic information is not sufficiently different from other types of health-related information to deserve special protection or other exceptional measures. The Committee denied genetic exceptionalism, meaning that genetic information does not differ sufficiently from other health-related information to warrant special protection.

Thomas Murray, the chair of the commitee, admits that the committee's decision was a reluctant one, but he seems to be able to address the fears of the critics. Murray uses the term "genetic prophecy" to describe the fear that a genetic profile is an unchangeable future diary. He does not find this justification for genetic exceptionalism compelling. According to Murray, genetic information is "neither unique nor distinctive" in its capacity for providing a look into the future. Further, Murray contends that genetic information is not alone in serving as a basis for discrimination. For instance, insurers use evidence of both current and future disease, genetic or nongenetic. Murray suggests that the public fears discrimination mostly on the basis of genetic information, over which we have no control, and of which we are largely unaware. In the end, the task force "concluded that there was no good moral justificaton for treating genetic information, genetic diseases, or genetic risk factors as categorically different from other medical information, diseases, or risk factors.". . .

Using DNA in Tort Cases

Because this discussion revolves around the discovery of genetic evidence in civil cases, it seems most likely that a tort case would be the appropriate civil case to utilize genetic information. As such, the tort system demands that the most equitable result be obtained. To the extent that genetic evidence is probative and reliable, it should be discoverable and used to achieve the most fair award. . . .

I propose that, along with discovery of a plaintiff's medical records and lifestyle information, plaintiffs should be required to submit to genetic testing if the tests may reveal useful information in calculating lifetime-damage awards.

In tort claims, a defendant can learn of the plaintiff's medical history simply by discovering the plaintiff's medical records. [Under laws and rules of evidence a party can "discover" or learn about certain facts, documents, witnesses, or other evidence known or available to other parties, unless they are privileged or otherwise exempt from discovery (nondiscoverable).] The Federal Rules of Civil Procedure provide that all nonprivileged material relevant to a claim in a lawsuit is discoverable. Often the plaintiff will bring a claim that places some confidential information at issue. Thus, courts often order the discovery of medical records, including some records that contain information protected by statute.

In contested cases, the courts can order privileged records discoverable if there is a "showing of good cause." Furthermore, in the discovery of substance-abuse records, the court can assess good cause by "weigh[ing] the public interest and the need for disclosure against the injury to the patient to the physician-patient relationship, and to the treatment services."

The courts seem willing to make privileged information available to defendants in circumstances that merit the concomitant intrusion upon privacy. Although courts often allow the discovery of medical records, they differ on their requirements for what types of circumstances require this intrusion. . . .

Predicting the Future

I propose that, along with discovery of the plaintiff's medical records and lifestyle information, plaintiffs should be required to submit to genetic testing if the tests may reveal useful information in calculating lifetime-damage awards. When plaintiffs try to recover on claims that require a lifetime-expectancy calculation, it seems to be the best application of genomic evidence and cost efficiency to expose plaintiffs to a multipanel blood test. The multipanel blood test could screen for a number of known genetic disorders that result from a monogenic mutation but do not appear until later in life. This would exclude some of the more common diseases, such as cancer, but environmental factors, along with genetic predispositions, cause cancer, a polygenic disorder. While excluding some of the more common diseases, the panel of tests would also exclude increased speculation currently inherent in the future determinations of polygenic diseases. A panel of tests revealing known, monogenic diseases that occur later in life would present an accurate picture of the future health of plaintiffs' lives. Therefore, the introduction of genomic evidence would allow for calculation of a more accurate damage award. . . .

Genetic evidence also can be used to demonstrate an individual's susceptibility to disease as a result of toxic exposure. This might lead to discourse on whether the manufacturer or employer has a "duty to protect hyper-sensitive individuals" and at what cost to the rest of society. The concept of recovery for latent risk stands to gain considerably from genetic evidence because biomarkers of disease precursors would either alleviate concerns about fraudulent or speculative claims, or confirm the plaintiff's concern and need for medical monitoring. Further, a defendant will argue assumption of risk as an affirmative defense if the plaintiff knows about his genetic susceptibilities and engages in injurious conduct nonetheless.

Within the legal system, the courts must face genetic evidence as the newest scientific advance and embrace it for the information it can provide.

In conclusion, "a blanket prohibition on use of plaintiffs" genetic data in tort cases seems ill-advised, given that the information will often be directly relevant to the issues in contention, and may in different cases help plaintiffs as often as it benefits defendants. . . .

In the Interests of Fairness and Justice

The future is upon us, and we as individuals must face our fears about the information our genes contain and how that information can affect us. Within the legal system, the courts must face genetic evidence as the newest scientific advance and embrace it for the information it can provide. Genetic evidence currently aids in adjudicating criminal and paternity contests, however, its potential reaches much further. Once courts confront the fears of using genetic evidence in civil cases, the parties will benefit from more accurate claim adjudication, whether in calculating lifetime expectancy damages or proving legal causation. Further, society's fears of genetic material will be assuaged. Our court system has the ability to persuade public opinion in this matter, and the time has come for courts to solidly support the use of scientific evidence in the courtroom, assuming the evidence is reliable and relevant to the matter at hand.

8

Genetic DNA Databases That Identify Donors Create High Risks of Abuse

Patricia A. Roche and George J. Annas

Both Patricia Roche and George Annas are professors in the Department of Health Law, Bioethics, and Human Rights at Boston University School of Public Health in Boston.

The analysis of DNA material, combined with Internet accessibility, creates an unregulated market in DNA peddling. It also creates new opportunity for invasion of genetic privacy. Once contained within the purview of the scientific and/or government community, the technology is now within the hands of private companies that collect and analyze samples and personal information for the express purpose of selling them to researchers. Private DNA is not like a credit card that can be surrendered for a new one with a different number. All consumers should lobby for a federal genetic privacy law to protect those who want to know what their DNA contains, as well as those who do not want to know, or do not want others to know.

"Who am I?" has always been a fundamental philosophical question that may require decades of reflection to answer. With the advent of DNA analysis, there is a growing public impression that the answer may be found in our genes. Various Internet sites offer descriptions of our ancestral history on the basis of our DNA, as well as testing for specific

Patricia A. Roche and George J. Annas, "DNA Testing, Banking, and Genetic Privacy," *The New England Journal of Medicine*, vol. 355, August 10, 2006, pp. 545–546. Reproduced by permission.

"disease genes" or general profiles that are used to recommend lifestyle changes, such as foods to be eaten or avoided. Researchers have even suggested that although the scientific evidence is speculative and at best probabilistic, many people will want to have their DNA analyzed for markers of predispositions toward certain behaviors, including risk taking, overeating, aggression, and even criminality.

Caution Is Warranted

As these opportunities to learn about our DNA expand and affect the way we construct our personal identities, we should be alert to the risks as well as the benefits of exploring our DNA and basing an understanding of who we are on genetic testing. We should be wary of perceptions of ourselves— whether our own or others'—that are based on results of tests that have not been validated or on misinterpretations of valid tests. We should be at least as concerned that others may know more than we do about our own genetic makeup. DNA analysis, in combination with the Internet, creates an unregulated market in DNA and new opportunities for invasions of genetic privacy.

Using the Internet for the marketing and purchasing of genetic tests sidesteps the doctor–patient relationship and eliminates meaningful, face-to-face genetic counseling. It also magnifies an older but unresolved danger: whenever identifiable DNA samples are collected and stored, there is a high risk that violations of genetic privacy will follow. As the evolution of DNA banking for research demonstrates, DNA donors shouldn't assume that the privacy protections they take for granted in medical care and clinical research apply. People give up more than they realize when they hand over their DNA.

DNA collection and banking have already gone through two distinct stages. Initially, the people most actively involved in DNA collection (outside law enforcement and the U.S.

military, both of which use DNA for identification purposes only) were researchers seeking genetic markers for a particular disease, who typically collected DNA samples from families at risk for the disease of interest and stored those samples. Consent forms typically contained a provision permitting the researchers to retain and reanalyze DNA samples in related research after the primary study was completed. In the next iteration, consent documents included much broader statements in which subjects acknowledged that their DNA samples would become the property of the researchers (or institutions), who could control the samples for their own benefit. The research subject was thereby transformed into a DNA donor.

The best consumer advice, given current law, is that one should not send a DNA sample to anyone who does not guarantee to destroy it on completion of the specified test.

In the Hands of Private Companies

Recent years have seen the emergence of private companies, such as the Ardais Corporation and DNA Sciences, that—either at hospitals or through appeals over the Internet—collect and analyze samples and personal information for the express purpose of selling them to researchers. The National Institutes of Health also has plans to develop a national repository similar to the U.K. Biobank, a new resource for researchers that will eventually include information and blood samples from 500,000 volunteers. With such developments, DNA banking is quickly changing from an academic research activity to a governmental and commercial enterprise conducted by DNA brokers. As a result, the relationship between subjects and researchers is being severed, and along with it the associated legal rights and obligations, including obligations to reduce risks to subjects' privacy and to maintain the confidentiality of their information. The unresolved legal status of the relationships among donors, brokers, and researchers raises troubling questions about privacy and property rights.

Without adequate protections for genetic privacy, autonomy to discover and use one's own genetic information for one's own purposes cannot be realized. A fundamental concern is that the possession and storage of a personally identifiable DNA sample give the possessor access to a wealth of information about the person and his or her genetic relatives. This includes information derivable from new DNA tests that were not available, or even anticipated, when the sample was relinquished. Consequently, as long as personally identifiable DNA samples are stored, there is the possibility of unauthorized access to and use of genetic information—an invasion of genetic privacy. To the extent that we see ourselves and our future as influenced by our genes, such invasions can disrupt our very sense of self.

In response to this concern, a majority of states have begun to regulate genetic testing and fair uses of genetic information. But these laws are almost exclusively antidiscrimination statutes that target the behavior of insurers, employers, or both after the DNA has been collected and analyzed. Some states, such as New Jersey, include broader privacy protections by prohibiting unconsented-to collection and testing of DNA generally (although those statutes typically include broad exceptions for law enforcement and medical research) and by defining requirements for consent to testing. Only about half a dozen states, however, require either explicit consent for sample storage or the destruction of samples after the purpose for their collection has been achieved.

It is, of course, the DNA sample itself, which can usefully be viewed as a coded probabilistic [assigned a value based upon the likelihood of developing a disease or condition] medical record, that makes genetic privacy unique and differentiates it from the privacy of medical records. The absence of any meaningful property or privacy protection of DNA samples means that consumers must be extra cautious and seek specific information about the fate of the samples before sending them off for testing. Minimal information that they should obtain includes the site where the sample will be analyzed, whether and how long it will be stored, and who will have access to it and to any identifiable information linked to it. The best consumer advice, given current law, is that one should not send a DNA sample to anyone who does not guarantee to destroy it on completion of the specified test.

Redefining ourselves and our futures in accordance with insights offered by our DNA is hopelessly reductionistic, if inherently fascinating. We will not learn who we are by having our DNA analyzed, but we will almost certainly give others the opportunity to learn something about us. And our DNA is not like our credit cards: we cannot simply get a new number. As long as someone has our identifiable DNA sample, he or she will be able to learn things about us we may not know, may not want to know, and certainly don't want others to know. DNA collection, banking, and analysis are expanding rapidly, and we need a federal genetic privacy law to protect people who want to know what secrets their DNA contains, as well as those who don't.

9

DNA Databases Allow Governmental Intrusion on Private Information

Gary T. Marx

Gary T. Marx is professor emeritus of sociology at M.I.T. and the author of several books on surveillance and society.

In an environment thick with concern about crime and terrorism, governments increasingly rely on "soft" means to collect personal information from individuals. When it comes to volunteering DNA samples (e.g., a mouth swab), the request appears just shy of harmless when compared to other, more seemingly intrusive requests, such as for urine, blood, or a pat-down probe or physical search. But therein lies the danger. When such a request is accompanied with appeals to good citizenship or patriotism, or the needs of the community relative to the rights of an individual, the voluntary compliance becomes subtly mandatory. Persons need to overcome the polite tendency to acquiesce when inappropriately asked to provide personal information, which, in fact, may constitute a softer form of secret or manipulative control of their personal liberties.

In Truro, Massachusetts, at the end of 2004, police politely asked all male residents to provide a DNA sample to match with DNA material found at the scene of an unsolved murder. Residents were approached in a non-threatening manner and asked to help solve the crime. This tactic of rounding up all the usual suspects and then some is still rare in the United States for historical, legal, and logistical reasons, but it is becoming more common. The Truro case illustrates expanding trends in surveillance and social control.

There is increased reliance on "soft" means for collecting personal information. In criminal justice contexts these means involve some or all of the following: persuasion to gain voluntary compliance, universality or at least increased inclusiveness, and emphasis on the needs of the community relative to the rights of the individual.

As with other new forms of surveillance and detection, the process of gathering the DNA information is quick and painless, involving a mouth swab, and is generally not felt to be invasive. This makes such requests seem harmless relative to the experience of having blood drawn, having an observer watch while a urine drug sample is produced, or being patted down or undergoing a more probing physical search.

In contrast, more traditional police methods, such as an arrest, a custodial interrogation, a search, a subpoena, or traffic stop, are "hard." They involve coercion and threat to gain involuntary compliance. They may also involve a crossing of intimate personal borders, as with a strip or body-cavity search. In principle such means are restricted by law and policy to persons there are reasons to suspect, and thus they implicitly recognize the liberty of the individual relative to the needs of the community.

Yet the culture of social control is changing. Hard forms of control are not receding, but soft forms are expanding. I note several forms of this, from requesting volunteers based on appeals to good citizenship or patriotism to using disingenuous communication to profiling based on lifestyle and consumption to utilizing hidden or low-visibility, information collection techniques. . . .

Painless Consent

Many forms of voluntarism are encouraged by techniques designed to be less directly invasive. Computers scan dispersed personal records for suspicious cases, avoiding, at least initially, any direct review by a human. Similarly X-ray and scent machines "search" persons and goods for contraband without touching them. Inkless fingerprints can be taken without the stained thumb symbolic of the arrested person. Classified government programs are said to permit the remote reading of computers and their transmissions without the need to directly install a bugging device.

Beyond the case of gathering DNA, consider the change from a urine drug test requiring an observer, to drug tests that require a strand of hair, sweat, or saliva. Saliva is particularly interesting. Whatever can be revealed from the analysis of blood or urine is also potentially found (although in smaller quantities) in saliva—not only evidence of disease and DNA, but also of drugs taken and pregnancy. The recent development of non-electrical sensors now makes it possible to detect molecules at minute levels in saliva.

To take blood is to pierce the body's protective armor. But expectorating occurs easily, frequently, and is more "natural" than puncturing a vein. Nor does it involve the unwanted observation required for a urine drug sample. Saliva samples can be taken easily and endlessly, and the changes charted in them make possible the early identification of problems.

More Uses than First Considered

This may offer medical diagnostic advantages to the individual. Diagnostic spitting as a condition of employment is obviously of interest to employers concerned with rising health costs and resistance to urine drug tests—and eager to avoid liability for the illnesses of those who work around hazardous chemicals.

Authorities concerned with identifying those who spit when not requested to can also use the technology. The transit authority in Sheffield, England, as part of an anti-spitting campaign, distributed three thousand DNA swab kits to transportation staff. Posters proclaim "Spit? It's Out" and warn persons who spit that ". . . you can be traced—and prosecuted. Even if we don't know what you look like. And your record will be on the national DNA database. Forever."

The automated analysis of urine offers many of the advantages of saliva. A diagnostic test routinely used in some Japanese employment contexts requires that each employee who enters a stall be identified through an access card. This permits a comprehensive record of flushed offerings over time. It is said to be of great benefit in the early diagnosis of health problems, and it can also determine drug use, recent sexual activity, and pregnancy.

A person's DNA can be collected from a drinking glass or from discarded dental floss.

In many of these cases citizens are at least informed of what is going on, even if the meaning of their consent is open to question. More troubling is the development of tactics that need not rely on the subject's consenting or even being informed. New hidden or low-visibility technologies increasingly offer the tempting possibility of bypassing awareness, and thus any need for direct consent, altogether.

New technologies overcome traditional barriers, such as darkness or walls. Night-vision technology illuminates what darkness traditionally protected (and the technology is itself protected, unlike an illuminated spotlight). Thermal imaging technology applied from outside can offer a rough picture of a building's interior based on heat patterns. There is no need for the observer to enter the space.

Sampling from Abandoned or Unanticipated Sources

A person's DNA can be collected from a drinking glass or from discarded dental floss. Facial-scanning requires only a tiny lens. Smart machines can "smell" contraband, eliminating the need for a warrant or for asking subjects for permission to invade their olfactory space or "see" through their clothes and luggage. Beyond the traditional reading of visual clues offered by facial expression, there are claims that the covert analysis of heat patterns around the eyes and of tremors in the voice and the measurement of brain wave patterns offer windows into feelings and truth telling. The face still remains a tool for protecting inner feelings and thoughts, but for how long?

Individuals need not be informed that their communications devices, vehicles, wallet cards, and consumer items increasingly will have RFID (Radio Frequency Identification) chips embedded in them that can be designed to be passively read by unseen sensors from up to thirty feet away.

In the convoluted logic of those who justify covert (or non-informed) data collection and use, individuals "volunteer" their data by walking or driving on public streets or entering a shopping mall; by failing to hide their faces or wear gloves or encrypt their communications; or by choosing to use a phone, computer, or a credit card. . . .

Meaningful Consent

In an environment of intense concern about crime and terrorism and a legal framework generated in a far simpler time, the developments discussed above are hardly surprising. Democratic governments need to be reasonably effective and to maintain their legitimacy (even as research on the complex relationships between effectiveness and legitimacy is needed). Working together and sacrificing a bit of oneself for the common good, particularly in times of crisis, is hardly controversial. Relative to traditional authoritarian settings, many of the above examples show respect for the person in offering notice and some degree of choice and in minimizing invasiveness. Such efforts draw on the higher civic traditions of democratic participation, self-help, and community. They may also deter. Yet there is something troubling about them. . . .

To be meaningful, choice should imply genuine alternatives and refusal costs that are not wildly exorbitant. Absent that, we have trickery, double-talk, and inequitable relationships. When we are told that for the good of the community we must voluntarily submit to searches or provide information, we run the danger of the tyranny of turning presumptions of innocence upside down. If only the guilty need worry, why bother with a Bill of Rights and other limits on authority? There also comes a point beyond which social pressure seems unreasonable. If the case for categorical information is strong, then the law ought to require it without need of the verbal gymnastics of asking for volunteers or arguing that subjects are in fact taking voluntary action in the full meaning of the term, when they aren't.

> We value privacy not to protect wrongdoing, but because an appropriate degree of control over personal and social information is central to our sense of self, autonomy, and material well-being.

Those who fail to volunteer can be viewed as having something to hide or as being bad citizens. The positive reasons for rejecting such requests are ignored. Yet we all have things to hide or, more properly, to reveal selectively, depending on the relationship and context. The general social value we place on sealed first-class letters, window blinds, and bathroom doors, and our opposition to indiscriminate wiretapping, bugging, and informing, or to giving up anonymity in public places (absent cause), are hardly driven by an interest in aiding the guilty. Sealing juvenile criminal records does not reflect a perverse strategy for infiltrating miscreants into adult life, but rather an understanding of, and some compassion for, the mistakes of youth.

What Is at Stake

We value privacy not to protect wrongdoing, but because an appropriate degree of control over personal and social information is central to our sense of self, autonomy, and material well-being—as well as being necessary for independent group actions. A healthy, if necessarily qualified, suspicion of authority is also a factor in restricting information sought by the more powerful. As consumers and citizens we have an interest in avoiding the manipulation, discrimination, and theft that can flow from combining bits of personal information that are innocuous by themselves.

Many of the new controls may seem more acceptable (or at least are less likely to be challenged) because they are hidden or built-in and less invasive relative to the traditional forms of crossing personal and physical borders. We are also often complicit in their application—whether out of fear, convenience, or for frequent-shopper awards. Converting privacy to a commodity in which the seller receives something in return to compensate for the invasion is a clever and defensible means of overcoming resistance.

Exchanges and less invasive searches are certainly preferable to data rip-offs and more invasive searches. However, the nature of the means does not determine its acceptability. What matters most is the appropriateness of collecting the information and only secondarily the way that it is collected. A search is still a search, regardless of how it is carried out. The issue of searches and the crossing of traditional borders between the civil and state sectors or the self and others involves much more than painless, quick, inexpensive (or positively rewarding), and non-embarrassing means.

Other factors being equal, soft ways are to be preferred to hard, even if the control/instrumental goals of those applying the surveillance remain the same. Yet coercion at least has the virtue (if that's what it is) of letting the subject (or object) know what is happening. What we don't know can hurt us as well.

Easier but Maybe Unwarranted

There are also pragmatic issues: does the tactical work? I have found no cases where the request for voluntarily offered samples solved the case. A guilty person would have to be very stupid indeed to come forth and volunteer a DNA sample. In the Truro case, a suspect was eventually arrested, but the arrest was based on other evidence.

Traditionally (if accidentally) there was a happy overlap between three factors that limited searches and protected personal information. The first was logistical. It was not cost- or time-effective to search everyone. The second was law. More invasive searches were prohibited or inadmissible, absent cause and a warrant. The third reflected the affront experienced in our culture when certain personal borders were involuntarily crossed (for example, strip and body-cavity searches, taking body fluids, and to a lesser degree, fingerprinting). Limited resources, the unpleasantness of invasive searchers (for both the searched and the searcher), and the ethos of a democratic society historically restricted searches.

These supports are no longer overlapping. Instead, they are being undermined by the mass media's encouragement of fear and perceptions of crises and by the seductiveness of consumption—together with the development of inexpensive, less invasive, broad searching tools. . . .

There is a chilling drift into a society where you have to provide ever-more personal information in order to prove that you are the kind of person who does not merit even more intensive scrutiny. Here we confront the insatiable information appetite generated by scientific knowledge in a risk-adverse society. In such a society, knowing more may only serve to increase the need for more information.

My concern is more with cultural and behavioral developments than with the law. . . .

The cultural changes are worrisome because they are diffuse, subtle, and unseen—and they often reflect choices that are difficult to challenge in a democratic society. The possibility of wrongful choice is an inherent risk of democracy.

One's liberty can be used to smoke, eat rich foods, drive environmentally unfriendly cars, and watch unreality television, as well as to volunteer personal information—whether to government or the commercial sector. A bad law can be challenged in court or repealed. A dangerous technology can be banned, regulated, or countered with a different technology. But the only way to respond to liberty-threatening choices of the kind discussed here is through dialogue and education (tools that are already disproportionately available to those supporting the current developments). . . .

No Easy Answers

There is no single answer to how the new personal information collection techniques ought to be viewed and what, if anything, should (or can) be done about them. From genuine to mandatory voluntarism and from open to secret data collection—these are points on continuums. There are important moral differences between what can be known through the unaided senses and what can only be known through technologically enhanced senses. The moral and practical issues around the initial collection of information are distinct from its subsequent uses and protections.

Diverse settings—national security, domestic law enforcement, public order maintenance, health and welfare, commerce, banking, insurance, public and private spaces and roles—do not allow for the rigid application of the same policies. The different roles of employer-employee, merchant-consumer, landlord-renter, police-suspect, and health provider-patient involve legitimate conflicts of interests. Any social practice is likely to involve conflict of values.

We need a situational or contextual perspective that acknowledges the richness of different contexts, as well as the multiplicity of conflicting values within and across them.

In the face of the simplistic rhetoric of polarized ideologues in dangerous times, we need attention to trade-offs and to the appropriate weighing of conflicting values. There is no fixed golden balance point. However the procedures for accountability and oversight so central to the founding and endurance of the country must remain strong. We must resist the appeals to morality and panic that can erode these procedures.

We need to overcome the polite tendency to acquiesce when we are inappropriately asked for personal information.

It would be foolish to elevate consent to an absolute, but neither should we continue to slide into a world where meaningful consent is only of historical interest. At best we can hope to find a compass rather than a map and a moving equilibrium rather than a fixed point for decision making.

Appreciating complexity is surely a virtue, but being immobilized by it is not. The default position should be meaningful consent, absent strong grounds for avoiding it. Consent involves participants who are fully aware of the surveillance system's presence and potential risks and of the conditions under which it operates. Consent obtained through deception or unreasonable or exploitative seduction or to avoid dire consequences is hardly consent. The smile that accompanies the statement, "an offer you can't refuse" reflects that understanding.

Just Say No

We must demand a principle of truth in volunteering; it is far better to say clearly that "as a condition of [entering here, working here, receiving this benefit, etc.] we require that you provide personal information." A golden rule principle ought also to apply: Would the information collector be comfortable in being the subject, rather than the agent, of surveillance, if the situation were reversed?...

We need to overcome the polite tendency to acquiesce when we are inappropriately asked for personal information. We need to just say "no" when, after we pay with a credit card, a cashier asks for a phone number or when a Web page or warranty form asks for irrelevant personal information or a video store seeks a Social Security number. Offering disinformation may sometimes be appropriate. The junk mail I receive for Groucho and Karl gives me a laugh as well as a way to track the erroneous information I sometimes provide.

Finally, technology needs to be seen as an opportunity, rather than a problem. Technologies can be designed to protect personal information and notify individuals when their information is collected or has been compromised....

Once a technology becomes widely available and is well known, responsibility for protection shifts legally (as well of course as practically) to the individual, not to those who would cross personal borders. In failing to act in response to changed circumstances beyond his or her control, the individual is seen to be making a choice and, in a sense, volunteering to be searched.

This blame-the-victim *caveat subjectus* [citizen beware] logic cries out for a cartoon entitled, "Where will it end?" Beyond the paper shredder, which has become routine in many homes, the cartoon would show a citizen protecting privacy by always wearing gloves, a mask, and perfume; having a closely shaved head; talking in code and encrypting all communications; insulating home, office, and packages in thermalimage-resistant tinfoil; and only using restrooms certified to be monitor free.

Now a Reality

[Novelist] Sinclair Lewis hoped in 1935 that *It Can't Happen Here*. But of course it can, and in some ways it has. Twenty years ago in reflections on the year and book *1984*, I wrote:

> The first task of a society that would have liberty and privacy is to guard against the misuse of physical coercion by the state and private parties. The second task is to guard against the softer forms of secret and manipulative control. Because these are often subtle, indirect, invisible, diffuse, deceptive, and shrouded in benign justifications, this is clearly the more difficult task.

Two decades later the hot-button cultural themes of threat, civil order, and security that Lewis emphasized are in greater ascendance and have been joined by the siren calls of consumption. If our traditional notions of liberty disappear, it will not be because of a sudden coup d'état. Nor will the iron technologies of industrialization be the central means. Rather, it will occur slowly, with an appeal to traditional American values in a Teflon- and sugar-coated technological context of low visibility, fear, and convenience.

10

Government Databases Have More Information than Needed to Solve Crimes

Electronic Privacy Information Center (EPIC)

The Electronic Privacy Information Center (EPIC) is a public interest research center, expressly established to focus public attention on pending or emerging civil liberties issues, especially those involving personal privacy. The organization provides policy and position statements and/or legal amicus *briefs (arguments submitted for the court's consideration by persons or entities who are not parties to the litigation, but who have a strong interest or concern in the subject matter at issue) for use in motions and appellate briefs in federal and state courts.*

The DNA material contained in national databases maintained by the Federal Bureau of Investigation (FBI) contains far more information about a person than a fingerprint. What was once considered "junk DNA" now appears to reveal personal genetic traits such as gender, race, ethnicity, and susceptibility to certain diseases or disorders. Moreover, a single DNA sample implicates not only the sample donor, but also the donor's family. The resulting genetic surveillance of both donor and family members raises serious privacy concerns, because it can be used for purposes unrelated to identification or crime solving.

The FBI maintains a national DNA database known as the Combined DNA Indexing System (CODIS). The FBI Laboratory's CODIS program allows federal, state, and local

Electronic Privacy Information Center (EPIC), *amicus curiae* brief filed in the case of *Johnson v. Quander*, on appeal to the U.S. Supreme Court from the U.S. Circuit Court of Appeals for the District of Columbia, filed June 30, 2006.

crime laboratories to collect, exchange and compare DNA profiles electronically. The FBI has selected short tandem repeat (STR) technology to generate profiles for CODIS. STR technology is used to evaluate 13 specific regions, known as loci or markers, within DNA located in a cell's nucleus. The 13 STR loci are located within "junk DNA," or DNA with no currently known function. . . .

CODIS could easily be a database of meaningful genetic traits, even if those traits are not currently known.

DNA Is More Personal than a Fingerprint

The use of DNA profiles in law enforcement is sometimes likened to the use of traditional fingerprints because both a fingerprint and a DNA profile are compared with evidence collected from a crime scene to determine whether there are matching identifying features. However, the information that can be obtained from a DNA sample is far more extensive than that from a fingerprint. DNA can provide information about a person's race, ethnicity, or even susceptibility to certain diseases. According to the Human Genome Project, coordinated by the Department of Energy and National Institutes of Health to map and study the entire human genetic sequence:

> DNA profiles are different from fingerprints, which are useful only for identification. DNA can provide insights into many intimate aspects of a person and their families including susceptibility to particular diseases, legitimacy of birth, and perhaps predispositions to certain behaviors and sexual orientation. This increases the potential for genetic discrimination by government, insurers, employers, schools, banks, and others.

Furthermore, "there is a chance that a person's entire genome may be available—criminal or otherwise. Although the

DNA used is considered 'junk DNA'; . . . in the future this information may be found to reveal personal information such as susceptibilities to disease and certain behaviors.". . .

The DNA profiles entered into the CODIS database can also reveal the likelihood that an individual is of a particular race. Studies have revealed that the likelihood of a match between a Caucasian American sample and a random Caucasian American in a database is 45 times more likely than a match between the sample and a random African American.

These correlations highlight privacy considerations not implicated by fingerprints, since it now seems more likely that the DNA profiles may, in fact, represent functional genetic material. The "junk DNA" sections that were selected for CODIS purposes are called "junk" only because their function is unknown. Until recently, DNA's main purpose was thought to be providing instructions for the creation of proteins. This "coding" DNA was believed to be the operative part of DNA, and the amount of coding DNA was thought to correlate with the complexity of the organism. New research is finding, however, that this correlation was misplaced. "Noncoding DNA" is the "junk" DNA that is used for forensic DNA analysis. However, researchers are finding that, far from being evolutionary junk, it does have a function. For instance, researchers have identified sets of non-coding sequences that are likely to be implicated in genetic diseases. It is important to note also that these research results have been published within the last 5–10 years, and research is proceeding rapidly. CODIS could easily be a database of meaningful genetic traits, even if those traits are not currently known.

Implication of Family Members

Not only can a DNA profile reveal information about an individual, it can, unlike a fingerprint, implicate members of an individual's family. . . . Profile matches occur between individuals with sibling and parent-child relationships. Other close familial relationships can result in a profile match, though with less certainty. Such matches can result in situations in which individuals may be investigated by law enforcement merely for having a relative whose DNA was collected at a crime scene. This problem is likely to encourage the expansion of DNA profiles to include additional markers. . . .

The fact that DNA samples can be used for purposes unrelated to identification also raises the significant problem that the samples will be sought by others for purposes unrelated to the initial collection.

Familial searches are gaining viability in both theory and fact. . . . This new use, although not yet widespread, dramatically affects the privacy of the family of anyone whose DNA is collected and profiled for law enforcement databases. . . .

The potential for identifying family members using these familial searching methods places innocent people under "lifetime genetic surveillance." Not only does this implicate the privacy concerns of millions of innocent people, but the surveillance would also be strongly defined against race lines. The searches imposed on close, familial matches would therefore be defined by racial and social inequities.

Misusing DNA Samples for Unrelated Purposes

The fact that DNA samples can be used for purposes unrelated to identification also raises the significant problem that the samples will be sought by others for purposes unrelated to the initial collection. . . .

More than a decade ago, the National Academy of Sciences recommended that samples be destroyed "promptly" after analysis. The Academy stated that "retention of DNA samples creates an opportunity for misuses—i.e., for later testing to determine personal information. In general, the committee discourages the retention of DNA samples." The Academy stressed that "investigation of DNA samples or stored information for the purpose of obtaining medical information or discerning other traits should be prohibited, and violations should be punishable by law."

These privacy concerns have led some states to create limited protections for the samples. Only Wisconsin statutorily requires that samples be destroyed after the completion of the DNA analysis. California and Idaho provide that unused samples can be disposed if certain privacy precautions are taken, but do not require disposal.

Several other countries have also taken steps to reduce the risk of subsequent misuse of DNA samples. For example, under Australian law, crime victims, witnesses to a crime, and anyone who volunteers DNA for police use may limit the use of their DNA for certain purposes and request that it be destroyed. A crime suspect may also request destruction of his sample after a not guilty verdict or within two years of its acquisition if no charge is brought. A requester need only make his request in writing to the designated person in charge of request. New Zealand, Germany, Sweden, Denmark and the Netherlands currently require samples to be destroyed after the profile has been created. . . .

Retention vs. Destruction of Samples

In contrast, the U.S. Department of Justice is seeking to impose broad retention requirements absent federal authority. The FBI quality assurance standards for laboratories participating in CODIS state: "Where possible, the laboratory shall retain or return a portion of the evidence sample or extract." Thereby, specimens may be stored indefinitely in case a profile is challenged or testing technology improves. Additionally, the recent renewal of the Violence Against Women Act, signed into law Jan. 5, 2006, authorized permanent retention of certain DNA samples.

Likewise, some states provide for permanent retention or set minimums. For example, Arizona requires that biological samples be maintained for at least 35 years.

The vast amount of information contained within a raw tissue or blood sample, beyond the identifiers available in a DNA profile, amplify the privacy risks faced by those whose samples are retained. . . .

It is also conceivable that soon, if not already, scientists will request access to CODIS in what would serve as a preexisting goldmine of DNA data for their research.

The Need for Protection

Some states explicitly prohibit the use of DNA profiles for purposes other than law enforcement. Other states prohibit specific uses of the information, such as obtaining information on physical traits and predisposition to certain medical conditions. However, some states explicitly permit limited use of the DNA profiles or samples for medical research, academic or research purposes, or creating a statistical database. Thirteen states allow their DNA databases to be used for "other humanitarian purposes" and thirty-four states expressly allow the creation of a population statistical database—a database which allows for the analysis and interpretation of DNA profiles, albeit anonymous profiles.

It is also conceivable that soon, if not already, scientists will request access to CODIS in what would serve as a preexisting goldmine of DNA data for their research. With access to such information, the scientists will argue the potential benefit to humanity in studying gene patterns among those persons with a propensity for criminal activity. The National Institute of Justice clearly foresaw this situation:

As [CODIS] enlarges and if it is broadened to include persons convicted of a larger variety of crimes, it might be possible that statistical studies of the databases could reveal useful information. Inventive researchers may glean useful information of a statistical sort. At the same time, there would need to be protection against misuse or use by unauthorized persons.

11

The Government Has Taken Steps to Secure Privacy of Its DNA Databases

Department of Justice, Federal Bureau of Investigation (FBI)

The Federal Bureau of Investigation (FBI) was created in 1908 under the jurisdiction of the U.S. Department of Justice. Its primary mission is to protect and defend the United States against terrorist and foreign intelligence threats, as well as to uphold and enforce U.S. criminal laws. With a budget of nearly $6 billion annually, the FBI employs more than thirty thousand worldwide, and oversees a national DNA electronic database system with access to international files as well.

Pursuant to the Privacy Act of 1974, the FBI conducted a Privacy Impact Assessment (PIA) of its National DNA Index System (NDIS), which is the system containing DNA profile records and supported electronically by the automated Combined DNA Index System (CODIS). Public notice of the FBI's findings in the PIA (which approved its use of NDIS) was made in 2004, in addition to publication of specific measures the FBI has implemented to protect privacy of DNA information. For example, NDIS does not retain information sufficient for the NDIS custodian to personally identify a record by name or other personal identifier. Moreover, individuals may review their records by contacting the authorities that initially received the DNA samples. All DNA records are secured in a government facility with access limited to authorized persons only.

Department of Justice, Federal Bureau of Investigation (FBI), "Federal Bureau of Investigation Privacy Impact Assessment: National DNA Index System (DNS)," February 24, 2004.

The FBI's Senior Privacy Official has reviewed the National DNA Index System (NDIS), and taking into account the need for this system and the privacy risks and protections discussed herein, the FBI approves the FBI's use of this system. . . .

National DNA Index System (NDIS) is a system of DNA profile records input by criminal justice agencies (including state and local law enforcement agencies). The Combined DNA Index System (CODIS) is the automated DNA information processing and telecommunication system that supports NDIS. Pursuant to the DNA Identification Act of 1994 (DNA Act), certain categories of information must be collected: 1) DNA identification records of persons convicted of crimes; 2) Analyses of DNA samples recovered from crime scenes; 3) Analyses of DNA samples recovered from unidentified human remains; 4) Analyses of DNA samples voluntarily contributed from relatives of missing persons; and 5) known reference sample from missing persons. At state and local levels, in addition to the above specimen categories, state law determines what categories of specimens and what offenses may be included in the database. NDIS does not retain information that would allow the NDIS Custodian to personally identify the record by name or other personal identifier. Individuals seeking to review their records are directed to contact the Federal, State, or local authority that received the DNA sample to obtain instructions on how to access their records.

DNA profiles are stored electronically and searched for possible matches. Matches made between the Forensic and Offender Indexes provide investigators with the identity of the suspected perpetrator(s). Matches made among profiles in the Forensic Index can link crime scenes together to ascertain identifying serial offenders. Based on a match, police in multiple jurisdictions can coordinate their respective investigations, and share the leads they developed independently. After CODIS identifies a potential match, qualified DNA analysts in the laboratories responsible for the matching profiles contact each other to validate or refute the match. Access to the database will be granted only to Federal, State and local crime laboratories performing DNA analysis.

What Information Is to Be Collected?

The NDIS system contains agency identifiers representing the agency submitting the DNA profile; the specimen identification number; the DNA profile; and the name of the DNA personnel associated with the DNA analysis.

Why Is the Information Being Collected?

The information is being collected pursuant to the DNA Act which requires certain DNA categories be collected. This Act also formalized the FBI's authority to establish a national DNA Index System for law enforcement purposes. In order to carry out that authority, the FBI collects the aforementioned information to assist state and local labs in processing DNA profiles. These DNA profiles are then stored electronically and searched for possible matches.

What Is the Intended Use of the Information?

The information in NDIS is used to match DNA profiles with crime scenes and human remains (missing persons). DNA profiles are stored electronically and searched for possible matches. Matches made between the Forensic and Offender Indexes provide investigators with the identity of the suspected perpetrator(s). Matches made among profiles in the Forensic Index can link crime scenes together to ascertain identifying serial offenders. Based on a match, police in multiple jurisdictions can coordinate their respective investigations, and share the leads they developed independently. After CODIS/NDIS identifies a potential match, qualified DNA analysts in the laboratories responsible for the matching profile-contact each other to validate or refute the match.

With Whom Will the Information Be Shared?

Access to the database will be granted only to Federal, State and local crime laboratories performing DNA analysis. If a match is found, it will be shared with the Federal, state or local law enforcement investigating the crime or searching for the missing person.

What Notice or Opportunities for Consent Would Be Provided to Individuals Regarding What Information Is Collected and How That Information Is Shared?

NDIS consists of two primary areas of collection and retention of DNA profiles. The first, The Relatives of Missing Person[s] Index, consists of DNA records from the biological relatives of individuals reported missing. Inclusion in this index is strictly voluntary and the person contributing the sample is required to fill out a "Consent and Information Form" which sets forth the elements of the Privacy Act. All DNA profiles in the population file are anonymous and are used for statistical inferences. The data file does not contain personal information, nor any identifying association, to the donor.

All records are maintained in a secure government facility with access limited to only authorized personnel or authorized and escorted visitors.

The second primary area of collection and retention is the convicted offender index. No notice is given to convicted offenders about what is being collected and how it will be shared. Convicted offenders do not have the option of not consenting and Federal law authorizes the force necessary to obtain the sample. Those samples, consisting of DNA profiles originating from and associated with evidence found at crime scenes, are included in the Forensic Index (a part of NDIS). The Convicted Offender Index consists of DNA records from offenders convicted of qualifying federal and/or state crimes.

How Will the Information Be Secured?

All records are maintained in a secure government facility with access limited to only authorized personnel or authorized and escorted visitors. Physical security protections include guards and locked facilities requiring badges and passwords for access. Records are accessed only by authorized government personnel and contractors and are protected by appropriate physical and technological safeguards to prevent unauthorized access. Access to the database has been granted to Federal, state and local crime laboratories performing DNA analysis who meet the aforementioned standards.

Organizations to Contact

The editors have compiled the following list of organizations concerned with the issues debated in this book. The descriptions are derived from materials provided by the organizations. All have publications or information available for interested readers. The list was compiled on the date of publication of the present volume; the information provided here may change. Be aware that many organizations take several weeks or longer to respond to inquiries, so allow as much time as possible.

American Civil Liberties Union (ACLU)
125 Broad Street, 18th Floor, New York, NY   10004
(212) 549-2585
Web site: www.aclu.org

The ACLU is a public advocacy organization that works with courts, legislatures, and communities to promote and protect personal liberties and related constitutional rights. Its concerns regarding DNA databases focus on privacy and liberty issues.

American Society of Law, Medicine & Ethics (ASLME)
765 Commonwealth Avenue, Suite 1634, Boston, MA   02215
(617) 262-4990 • Fax (617) 437-7596
Web site: www.aslme.org

The ASLME is an educational organization of professionals in the allied fields of law, medicine, and ethics. It provides a forum for the exchange of information and research in an interdisciplinary setting. ASLME has undertaken a multi-year scholarly research project of ethical, legal, and social issues surrounding the use of forensic DNA profiling, in particular, its DNA Fingerprinting and Civil Liberties Project.

Electronic Privacy Information Center (EPIC)
1718 Connecticut Ave. NW, Suite #200
Washington, DC   20009
(202) 483-1140
Web site: www.epic.org

The Electronic Privacy Information Center (EPIC) is a public interest research center, expressly established to focus public attention on pending or emerging civil liberties issues, especially those involving personal privacy. The organization provides policy and position statements and/or legal *amicus* briefs (arguments submitted for the court's consideration by persons or entities who are not parties to the litigation, but who have a strong interest or concern in the subject matter at issue) for use in motions and appellate briefs in federal and state courts.

GeneWatch UK
The Mill House, Tideswell, Buxton
Derbyshire[irt1]   SK 17, 8LN
+44 (0) 1298 871898 • Fax +44 (0) 1298 872531
Web site: www.genewatch.org

GeneWatch UK is a not-for-profit group that monitors developments in the field of genetics from a public interest/environmental protection/animal welfare perspective. Its Web page is a forum for international resource links in the field of current issues involving DNA and genetic research in general.

Human Genome Project/National Human Genome Research Institute
National Institutes of Health, Bethesda, MD   20892-2152
(301) 402-0911 • Fax (301) 402-2218
Web site: www.genome.gov

The National Human Genome Research Institute led the Human Genome Project for the National Institutes of Health (NIH) (under the U.S. Department of Health and Human Services). Its research culminated in the completion of the full human genome sequence in 2003, and the knowledge gained from this project is expected to greatly enhance the fight against disease and the improvement of human health.

The Innocence Project
100 Fifth Avenue, 3rd Floor, New York, NY   10011
(212) 364-5340
Web site: www.innocenceproject.com

The Innocence Project was founded in 1992 at the Benjamin N. Cardozo School of Law at Yeshiva University, by Barry C. Scheck and Peter J. Neufield. It is a non-profit legal clinic and advocacy organization that pioneered the use of DNA tests to exonerate wrongfully-convicted persons. Under the auspices of law school professors and legal staff, law students generally take on either "cold cases" or cases in which post-conviction DNA testing can yield conclusive proof of innocence. As of early 2007, the organization has been instrumental in the exoneration of one-hundred and ninety convictees.

National Association of Criminal Defense Lawyers (NACDL)
1150 Eighteenth St. NW, Suite 950, Washington, DC   20036
(202) 872-8600
Web site: www.nacdl.org

The NACDL, with approximately thirteen thousand members nationwide, is the preeminent professional bar association representing U.S. criminal defense professionals. The organization provides policy and position statements and/or legal *amicus* briefs (arguments submitted for the court's consideration by persons or entities who are not parties to the litigation, but who have a strong interest or concern in the subject matter at issue) for use in motions and appellate briefs in federal and state courts.

U.S. Department of Justice, Federal Bureau of Investigation (FBI)
J. Edgar Hoover Building, Washington, DC   20535-0001
(202) 324-3000
Web site: www.fbi.gov

The Federal Bureau of Investigation (FBI) was created in 1908 under the jurisdiction of the U.S. Department of Justice. Its primary mission is to protect and defend the United States against terrorist and foreign intelligence threats, as well as to uphold and enforce U.S. criminal laws. With a budget of nearly $6 billion annually, the FBI employs more than 30,000 worldwide, and oversees a national DNA electronic database system with access to international files as well. According to the FBI, as of July 2006, its National DNA Index System (NDIS) contained 144,582 forensic profiles and 3,412,572 convicted offender profiles (www.fbi.gov/hq/lab/codis/national.htm).

U.S. Department of Justice (DOJ), National Commission on the Future of DNA Evidence
National Institute of Justice, Washington, DC   20531
(202) 307-9907
Web site: www.ojp.usdoj.gov

The National Commission on the Future of DNA Evidence was established by the National Institute of Justice (the research and development part of the U.S. Department of Justice) in 1998. Its original purpose was to advise the U.S. Attorney General on the use of current and future DNA methods within the criminal justice system, and to recommend policy and courses of action to improve the use of DNA in the investigation and adjudication of criminal cases.

Bibliography

Books

C.H. Asplen, et al. *National Forensic DNA Study Report.* Washington, DC: U.S. Department of Justice, 2003.

Cynthia Brown *Lost Liberties: Ashcroft and the Assault on Personal Freedom.* New York: New Press, 2003.

Nat Hentoff *The War on the Bill of Rights and the Gathering Resistance.* New York: Seven Stories Press, 2003.

Kevin M. Keenan *Invasion of Privacy: A Reference Handbook.* Santa Barbara, CA: ABC-CLIO, 2005.

Lawrence Kobilinsky, et al. *DNA: Forensic and Legal Applications.* Somerset, NJ: Wiley Interscience, 2004.

David Lazer, ed. *DNA and the Criminal Justice System: The Technology of Justice.* Cambridge, MA: MIT Press, 2004.

Dr. Henry Lee *Blood Evidence: How DNA is Revolutionizing the Way We Solve Crimes.* New York: Perseus, 2003.

Richard C. Leone *The War on Our Freedoms: Civil Liberties in an Age of Terrorism.* New York: Public Affairs, 2003.

National Institute of Justice	*Special Report: Using DNA to Solve Cold Cases.* Washington, DC: U.S. Department of Justice, 2002.
R.A. Pagon	"Uses of Databases," In: B. Korfe & L. Jorde, eds., *Encyclopedia of Genetics, Genomics, Proteomics, and Bioinformatics (chapter 99).* London, UK: Wiley, 2005.
Daniel J. Solove	*The Digital Person: Technology and Privacy in the Information Age.* New York: NYU Press, 2004.

Periodicals

Dwight E. Adams	"National DNA Database Is Well-Worth Taxpayers' Investment," *USA Today*, December 1, 2005.
American Civil Liberties Union (ACLU) Press Release	"ACLU Praises Charlottesville Police for Temporary Suspension of DNA Dragnet, Offers Advice for New Rules," April 15, 2004. Available at: http://achiva.org/newsreleases/2004/Apr15.html.
Seth Axelrad	"Special Report: Survey of State DNA Database Statutes," *American Society of Law, Medicine & Ethics*, 2005. Available at: www.aslme.org/dna-04/grid.index.php.
Marcello Ballve	"DNA Fingerprinting Trend Threatens Genetic Privacy," *Alternet*, July 14, 2004. Available at: www.alternet.org/rights/19234.

Frederick R. Bieber and David Lazer	"DNA Sweep Must be Accompanied by Informed Consent," *Provincetown (RI) Banner*, January 20, 2005.
Mildred K. Cho and Pamela Sankar	"Forensic Generics and Ethical, Legal and Social Implications Beyond the Clinic," *Nature Genetics Supplement*, November 2004.
Corrections Today	"DNA's Link to Corrections," October 2004.
Jared A. Feldman and Richard J. Katz	"Genetic Testing and Discrimination in Employment: Recommending a Uniform Statutory Approach," *Hofstra Lab. & Emp. Law Journal*, vol. 19, 2002.
Holly K. Fernandez	"Genetic Privacy, Abandonment, and DNA Dragnets: Is Fourth Amendment Jurisprudence Adequate?" *Hastings Center Report*, 2005.
Mark Hansen	"DNA Dragnet," *American Bar Association (ABA) Journal*, April 29, 2004.
Harvard Law Review	"Constitutional Law-Fourth Amendment-Ninth Circuit Upholds Collection of DNA from Parolees," December 2004.
Mark A. Jobling and Peter Gill	"Encoded Evidence: DNA in Forensic Analysis," *Nature Reviews Genetics*, vol. 5, issue 10, October 2004.
Elizabeth E. Joh	"Reclaiming 'Abandoned' DNA: The Fourth Amendment and Genetic Privacy," *Northwestern University Law Review*, Winter 2006.

D.H. Kaye and Michael E. Smith   "DNA Identification Databases: Legality, Legitimacy, and the Case for Population-Wide Coverage," *Wisconsin Law Review*, 2003.

Sally Lehrman   "Partial to Crime," *Scientific American*, December 2006.

Timothy W. Maier and Paul M. Rodriguez   "Inside the DNA Labs," *Insight on the News*, vol. 19, issue 13, 2003.

New Atlantis   "DNA Dragnets," Spring 2005. Available at: www.thenewatlantis.com

New Scientist   "Your DNA in Their Hands," April 9, 2005.

Sue Reid   "Do the Police Have Your Child's DNA?" *London Daily Mail*, January 21, 2006.

Rachel Ross   "A Trail of Genetic Evidence Follows Us All," *Toronto Star*, February 2, 2004.

K. Staley   "Genewatch UK, The Police National DNA Database: Balancing Crime Detection Human Rights and Privacy," Briefing Number 31, June 2005. Available at: www.genewatch.org/ HumanGen/Publications/Reports/ NationalDNADatabase.pdf

University of Washington   "Gene Tests," 2006. Available at: www.genetests.org

Lindsey Wade   "Facing the Threat: Invading the
                      Body for National Security," *Knowl-
                      edge, Technology, & Policy*, Spring
                      2004.

Jonathan Weems   "A Proposal for a Federal Genetic
                      Privacy Act," *Journal of Legal Medi-
                      cine*, Vol. 24, March 2003.

Marcia J. Weiss   "Beware! Uncle Sam Has Your DNA:
                      Legal Fallout from Its Use and Mis-
                      use in the U.S.," *Ethics and Informa-
                      tion Technology*, March 2004.

Richard Willing   "DNA Database Used to Help Solve
                      Thefts," *USA Today*, October 19,
                      2006.

Index